T H E
ONLY
ONE
I N T H E
ROOM

THE ONLY ONE IN THE ROOM

MILTON THOMPSON

CREATION
HOUSE

Design Director: Justin Evans
Cover design by Lisa McClure

Visit the author's Web sites: livingstonescharismatic.com and thompsonstories.com

Library of Congress Cataloging-in-Publication Data:
2016938850
International Standard Book Number: 978-1-62998-540-4
E-book International Standard Book Number:
978-1-62998-541-1

While the author has made every effort to provide accurate telephone numbers and Internet addresses at the time of publication, neither the publisher nor the author assumes any responsibility for errors or for changes that occur after publication.

First edition

16 17 18 19 20 — 9 8 7 6 5 4 3 2 1
Printed in Canada

CONTENTS

ACKNOWLEDGMENTS

I HAVE A LOT to be grateful for. Daily I thank God for what I have and the blessings and opportunities that have come my way. My life could have been a lot different had He not given me the family I have and the guidance I've received.

I want to thank God for making me who I am, including the race that I am. The history of the struggle of my people is not only a part of my DNA, but it has also been woven into my own narrative. Over the years as I have tried to find acceptance and my own place in the fabric of this nation, the struggle has left wounds, and as a result I have not always considered it a blessing to be black. But I've always been aware of God's guidance throughout multiple generations of my family.

God has been my anchor throughout my entire lifetime, and when my identity has been tossed to and fro I have found comfort and some degree of stability in His presence. His Word has also endowed me with a sense of purpose. For this I am eternally grateful to Him. The things I don't fully comprehend fall within the words of the apostle Paul in the New Testament: "For now we see through a glass darkly; but then face to face: now I know in part; but then shall I know even as also I am known" (1 Cor. 13:12, KJV).

I also want to acknowledge the key people who have made me who I am today. I have seen the anger of young black men who grew up without a father to help them make sense of the world, but I was blessed to have had two parents who loved me. Arzell and Mary Thompson are two people you will meet in this book. They worked hard to put food on the table and a roof over my head, always encouraging me to live a better life than they did. They provided stability and showed me what a family should be like. In my formative years no one impacted my thoughts and experiences about life and race more than my parents.

Like many people of my heritage, they endured hardship and displayed a humility that arose from their faith in the midst of the things that they suffered. Any degree of dignity that is displayed in our family derives from our parents' wisdom, common sense, and grit. They left the Jim Crow South, moved north, lived long lives, and left a legacy behind in their sons, Lewis, Linton, James, Arzell Jr., Stanley, and myself. Their old-fashioned discipline (with a switch) and a no-nonsense approach, though primitive by today's enlightened class, put the fear of God and a respect for others within us. They sacrificed much so that we could have the lives that we presently enjoy, and for this we are truly thankful.

I also want to thank God for my in-laws, Charles and Mavis Might. They welcomed me, a black man, into their white family during a time when interracial marriage was unconventional to say the least. When my wife, Peggy, asked her father about marrying me, he affirmed to his daughter, "Any son of Arzell Thompson is good enough to marry my daughter." I was young and in need of the guidance of many strong hands. Their belief in my potential supplemented that of my own parents and provided me with a "double portion." I acknowledge their encouragement and support, and someday I will thank them personally before the throne of grace.

Last of all I want to thank the most important person in my life: my wife. Peggy's parents took her to NAACP meetings when she was a young child in Ohio. They also intentionally enrolled her in schools that had black and Hispanic children during the 1950s. They instilled in her a sense of love, mercy, and justice toward all who suffer unjustly. Peggy has watched me go through a lifetime of wrestling with my identity as a black man in America, all the while comforting, strengthening, and encouraging me. She has watched me fight the rejection, self-doubt, and loneliness that have come with trying to find my way in a society that continues to struggle with race.

Though interracial marriage is not uncommon today, it was not so in 1976 when we first married. Peggy has endured the stares, ridicule, and hatred of those who wondered how she could marry someone of an "inferior group." She is my hero, though it has taken me awhile to realize that I have not been in this struggle alone.

INTRODUCTION

I F YOU PAY attention to our national conversation it's
no secret that the media steers that dialogue. Some
current events, like natural disasters, generate continual
coverage, while others, like the persecution of Christians,
are barely noticed. And then there are topics that rise and
fall because, frankly, the public becomes weary of talking
about them. Race is such a topic.

When I first started writing this book race was hardly
on the national radar screen. There was very little conversation about it. Then in 2014 Michael Brown was shot in
Ferguson, Missouri, by a white police officer. Eric Garner
died in New York after being placed in a chokehold by
police officers. Tamir Rice, a twelve-year-old boy, was
shot in Ohio when officers thought his pellet gun was a
real gun. Suddenly buildings were burning, cop cars were
demolished, and private businesses that people spent a
lifetime building were literally destroyed in minutes as a
result of rioting, violent demonstrations, and looting.

There were many groups that weighed in on the intolerable incidents that began to surface week after week. The
Black Lives Matter protests began as one such group and
quickly evolved into a national movement with no small
degree of controversy. They gained the national spotlight
when their demonstrations interrupted the speeches of
presidential candidates and stopped traffic in major cities.
While some saw this as a nuisance and questioned what

the fuss was about, I found their participation in the dialogue of race helpful.

Though I did not agree with the means, I know from experience that nothing changes unless it is kept at the forefront of the national conversation. That was true during the civil rights movement, and it's even more true in America today when keeping up with the news flow about racial conflicts is like navigating through whitewater rapids (no pun intended). The rushing waters wait for no one.

When violence was directed toward other races there were public figures who felt it necessary to interject that all lives matter. Although intended to deflect revenge, this seemed to minimize the black victims of police violence such as Walter Scott, who was shot in the back multiple times while fleeing a police officer in North Charleston, South Carolina. He was wanted for child support. This 2015 incident was caught on video and played over and over again on cable news. If the same incident happened frequently to white men who owed child support, then it would be a valid point. It does not.

America is seeing a resurgent civil rights movement of sorts, but will these events stimulate serious and difficult conversations that lead to progress, or will the focus soon be pushed out of the national conscience by another news story? Whether it's blaring in the headlines or buried in the obituaries, the story of race in America is here to stay.

Despite all the progress we've made in our country, including electing a black president, in today's politically correct climate it's getting harder and harder to have an honest, intelligent conversation about race. Some dance around the topic, preferring the safer talking points of poverty, demographics, and linguistic diversity as the reasons for the stalled progress of black people. They pontificate as to the reasons why "certain segments" of the population have experienced intergenerational poverty and a lack of opportunity, but they avoid discussions about racism, especially within the church—the most segregated element of our society. Others resort to bombastic rhetoric and name-calling, as is particularly evident in social media.

Like a virus, the subject of race has a pathology of its own, mutating into new forms, making it difficult to eradicate. I've heard conservative commentators such as Bill O'Reilly offer solutions, including the need for blacks to embrace the values of hard work and education and to stop having babies out of wedlock. While I am in complete agreement with him, it's much more complex than he realizes. Many black families have made little progress despite working hard for multiple generations.

Race is a subject that transcends generations. As a black child, I grew up with a keen awareness of my family's flight from the Jim Crow South to our attempted assimilation in the North. In my adult life, as a black man blessed with an interracial family, I have been as blind to the notion of race as bound to it. And as a black professional working in a white community I have wanted to both herald and hide from the subject.

I know I'm expected to bear no psychological turmoil from being black in America. Along with all my black friends from my generation I am expected to say, "I'm black and I'm proud." I *am* proud to be black and to have the heritage that I have been given, but that does not exclude me from the inner conflicts that come from being race conscious. If you are a black male, you have probably been impacted by race-based experiences more than you realize. I've come to discover they have left scars in me.

I am writing this book with the hope that it will help those who struggle with their racial identity as I do, and also that it will awaken the hearts of those who have no personal understanding of the pain racism inflicts. As I peel off the layers of memories and experiences that have shaped me over my lifetime, I share my deepest emotions of heart and soul. It's risky, I know, but I genuinely hope it will offer comfort, insight, and healing to those who have traveled the same journey and found few companions.

For others who have never walked this road, I pray it will allow you to see and feel the world from someone else's skin. If you are not black but you are a person of good will, I hope this book stimulates hard, uncomfortable conversations. Many have watched in trepidation when someone else was branded a racist for asking certain questions or venturing a particular opinion. This has intimidated them into silence, avoiding discussions on race. They have been silenced by some of the very people who should have welcomed their engagement in this type of discussion: black people. Whether their curiosity was born out of a sincere desire to know or out of sheer ignorance, their interest in talking about it should be embraced rather than rebuked.

The church is not exempt from this conversation. Rather than following Jesus' commands to love one another as He loves us (John 13:34), Sunday mornings continue to be the most segregated hour of the week in America, evidence that the roots of racism run deep among people of every color. As a Christian, I say this to our shame.

Having had various positions as a superintendent of schools and as a lover of history, I lend my views gleaned from a long career in education. However, this book is not meant to be a sociological or historical work, nor am I attempting to represent what *all* black people go through in coming to their own racial identities. I do not know, or even pretend to know, what all black people think or feel. Since mine are the only eyes through which I have seen the world, I can only give insight into the isolation and confusion of a single individual: Milton Bernard Thompson. The lenses that I look through are those of an African-American male raised in the North by southern parents during and beyond the civil rights era.

To understand my life and my psychological and spiritual makeup, you have to understand my parents, Arzell and Mary Thompson. This is not just a walk down memory lane. As we turn the pages of their life story together you will see how race dictated the events and course of their lives as well as my own. Although our journey together brings you along the hills and valleys of my own life, we will also travel the passages of my family's history, from my parents' faith-filled pilgrimage to my sons' modern-day struggles, to show you how much has and has not changed over three generations.

From time to time it will be impossible for me to avoid bringing a political perspective into my observations, so although you may be tempted to pigeonhole me, please resist that temptation. I tell you up front that I am filled with contradictions, enigmas, and inconsistencies. But if you allow me to share what I have seen and experienced regarding race in America from the late 1950s into the 2010s, your head will not only be challenged but your heart might just be undone.

As a Christ follower I share experiences I've had both within the church and outside of it. What this perspective brings to the topic is a faith that is powerful enough to keep a root of bitterness from springing up within me and defiling others. The writer of Hebrews 12:15 says, "Guard against turning back from the grace of God. Let no one become like a bitter plant that grows up and causes many troubles with its poison" (GNB). It also allows me to forgive people for things they have said or done to me that were deliberate, as well as those that were not. Some experiences and comments I've endured were mean-spirited, while others were unintentional gaffes borne of ignorance. As I was writing this book God brought a lot of hidden things to the surface—things that I'd *repressed* when they should have been *confessed*.

Although I discuss race honestly and with some emotion, let me be clear: I do not see racism around every corner, neither do I count every slight as a sign of racism. In the Bible, James writes, "For we all offend in many things" (James 3:2, JUB). Knowing this, I have fought hard to avoid feeling that everyone's intent is malicious, even when it results in hurt. It doesn't serve me to think that way, nor does it open doors of understanding with others.

Similarly, there must be an acknowledgment of progress in this country. We now live in a day when the election of the first black president occurred far sooner than I could have imagined, which speaks to the openness and goodwill of the majority of Americans. This shows a significant change from past attitudes and practices. In the past, whites did not have to meet *secretly* to limit the opportunities of black people; those shackles were embedded in the law, including the Constitution, which stated that black people were to be legally counted as only three-fifths of a person.

In this book I have chosen to refer to my people as *black people*. If I had chosen to use the term *African*

American I would have felt obligated to refer to every other American in hyphenated form. For instance, I am married to a German-American woman, I have friends who are Armenian-Americans, and I know people who are Oneida-Americans. Rather than being that specific, I use the terms *black* and *white* and a particular ethnic title when I am speaking of the immigrant groups that existed in my neighborhood growing up.

How do people define what constitutes a legitimate claim to membership in their ethnicity? It's interesting to learn what constitutes membership in the Oneida Indian Nation, for example. A person claiming Oneida heritage must present evidence to the tribal council, including proof of at least 25 percent of Oneida blood. It is not so clear-cut with others, however. With the increasing number of people of mixed heritage, it's not always easy to check the *black, white,* or *Asian* box on a form. My own children have an intriguing heritage of African, Native-American, and European blood, yet in this book I refer to them as black because that's how society recognizes them, at least at this current time.

Despite the fundamental religious beliefs of Christians, Jews, and Muslims, who all assert that mankind was born of one couple—Adam and Eve—the idea of racial inequality has been taught as fact since the late seventeenth century in America, where legal codes began restricting the rights of black people in some of the colonies. In the ancient world racial prejudice based upon color was an unknown concept. For instance, in ancient Rome people of all ethnicities and skin tones were slaves.

Today, however, the scientific community is actually beginning to debate the biological basis for race. Whether you believe in creation or evolution, as our understanding of DNA evolves it's pointing to the genetic sameness of our ancestors, begging the question "Is race even a thing?" That kind of scientific discussion is beyond the scope of this book, but even if race is nothing more than a societal or political construct, I maintain that it's a powerful one that significantly impacts our perceptions and behavior, especially in America.

Chapter 1
MY CONSTANT COMPANION

STEALTHILY ENTERING AN elementary classroom, I tiptoe past the artwork on the wall and steady myself on a little chair to watch the learning that's taking place. I figure if I crouch down and slouch my shoulders nobody will notice me, but the boys and girls stare at me, their faces showing surprise at the presence of a stranger. What am I thinking? I'm six feet four inches tall and two hundred and twenty-five pounds.

And I'm also black.

When I first became superintendent of schools in this mostly white community I thought I could visit the classrooms without distracting from the learning environment. But few of the children had interacted with black people on a regular basis, so I must have been in denial to think I could just sneak in unnoticed.

On my first visit to the lunchroom of one of our elementary schools I went from table to table saying hello to the children and teachers. As I approached one table, a young man looked up at me and his eyes lit up; he could barely contain his excitement.

"I know who *you* are!" he beamed.

"You do?" I asked, a little incredulous.

"You're the president!" he declared. I didn't know what to do, but I later told the staff that I'd apparently received a promotion!

A couple weeks later when I attended a family fun night at the middle school a student approached me declaring that I looked just like Morgan Freeman. Though I like Morgan Freeman, I was a little disappointed that I hadn't been mistaken for Denzel Washington.

The innocence of children is very refreshing in these humorous incidents, and I chalk it up to their attempt to fit someone new and different into a frame of reference they can understand. For them, it was the world of celebrity or entertainment. Outside of that, along with a large number of Americans, they've had little personal experience with black people.

I was born on May 26, 1953, in Racine, Wisconsin. I am on the back nine of my life, a fact that until recently I was not ready to admit. I find that as I've gotten older I've become more race conscious, and I'm more attuned to feelings of isolation in a profession where I've been the only black male in multiple situations.

As an educator I've worked up the professional ranks from advisory roles to superintendent of schools. The demographics have varied widely, but at this particular post I was one of only a handful of black people in the immediate area. I lived in an apartment in the town, I shopped at the local grocery store, and I ate in the local restaurants. I was almost always the only black person there, and although I tried not to be I was always conscious of standing out, of being different. Occasionally I would go shopping in a more diverse city nearby just to see people who looked more like me. It helped me let my guard down and just relax a bit more.

It was a solitary existence, compounded by the fact that my wonderful wife, Margaret (Peggy), stayed behind in our hometown about one hundred and seventy miles away, where we still owned a home, because she is not yet retired. Peggy is a schoolteacher.

And she's white.

During that time we saw each other on alternate weekends. Sometimes on Mondays my bags were packed in anticipation of going home to be with her on Fridays. We've been married for forty years, and we have four grown sons: Nathanael, Matthew, Thomas, and Daniel. When we all gather together for Christmas or for a few days in the summer, the conversations around our table are never dull.

Peggy and I met in our parents' church. With a German-American background, she is a daughter of the American Revolution, except her family fought on the wrong side in the war! Her ancestor, Georg Bingle, fought in the Revolutionary War but as a Hessian soldier. He was a paid mercenary for King George III of England. After the war he returned to Germany and told such wonderful stories about America that his three sons immigrated here. I'm so glad he did, otherwise I would never have met my soul mate. She will follow me anywhere, as long as I am also following the Lord; she has proven this over the years. There were difficult times when I took jobs away from home as a superintendent, but she's been steadfast, even in situations where other whites must have wondered why she married a black man. This was really evident in the seventies when we got married, but it rears its head from time to time even now.

An introvert in most social situations, Peggy summons the extroverted side of her personality at work. When she's with her students she's compassionate and in charge. And when she begins to talk about the things of God, it's like a switch is flipped, and her excitement for the Lord Jesus is unleashed.

As an educator and former pastor, I like people, but as

superintendent of schools it would have been nice to have the occasional luxury of camouflaging myself when I went out in the town because my role required me to make the occasional tough or controversial decisions. When I was new to town and first started attending district events everyone noticed I was there, but most people didn't seem aware that I was feeling like an outsider. I would enter the football stadium or the basketball gymnasium and look around for someone I knew, someone who could help me feel connected.

Tom was that guy. At our first home game I walked into the football stadium, and since I had only been on the job for about a month I hardly knew anyone. I didn't want to draw attention to myself, so I sat at the far end of the bleachers. At the next game I came in and decided to just sit there and watch the game, even if I was alone the whole evening. But Tom, a local chiropractor whom I had never met, walked over and invited me to sit with his family. I was glad to join them, and for the rest of the season I would enter the stadium looking for Tom. After football season, when I attended a few basketball games and wrestling matches, again I would walk into the gym hoping someone—maybe a staff member—might notice that I was alone. Usually it was Tom who invited me to sit with him. Because he used to live in Atlanta, Georgia, Tom was more comfortable with diversity and, frankly, more attentive to it.

Some time later, I had to make a difficult educational decision that affected Tom's daughter and her basketball team. My new friend was among a large group of people who showed up at the school board meeting to protest the decision. I had previously arranged to go to a game later that week with Tom and his family, but after the tense meeting I pulled him aside for a moment.

"Tom," I said, "I'm not going to make it to the game this week." He didn't seem to know what to say. "I'm willing to take responsibility for decisions that I made," I told him, "but I'm not a masochist who likes to walk into a place where people might be potentially hostile." I felt isolated enough, and that type of situation would just feed the race-consciousness I was fighting with, even though I knew it wasn't racially motivated.

I left that board meeting feeling really discouraged and wondering if I was the right fit for that school district. My job came with tough decisions, and I knew that. I realized they didn't protest my decision because of my race—that wasn't even a factor—but it didn't change how I felt.

I had been this kind of pioneer before. Growing up, I was the first black bag boy at a Kohl's food store in Racine. My brothers and I were some of the first black caddies at Meadowbrook Country Club there. I'd been placed in this situation time after time throughout the course of my life, and at times I've found it to be a tiresome experience.

The morning after the board meeting as I was walking down the hallway of my office building toward the front door I heard someone trying to buzz in. I looked closely, and it was Tom. I nervously let him in, thinking he was there to give me a piece of his mind since he didn't do so the night before.

"I've been thinking about you and just wanted to stop by and see how you're doing," Tom said. He was sincere. After talking for a few minutes we shook hands. Since I never felt like broaching the subject of race with Tom— since our friendship was based on mutual trust—Tom will never know what his simple gestures have done to make me feel welcome during times when I've felt estranged.

Often when I ate out at restaurants on weekends I had to dine alone. Although I was a high-profile member of the community and I liked to go out and meet people in the town, this caused some dissonance within me because I am a strange combination of introvert and extrovert. One day when I walked into a restaurant I was glad to see a coworker who was there with her family.

"Come and sit with us," she said with a friendly smile. At first I declined, but my coworker kindly insisted. "We don't mind," she assured me, so I joined them. As we were waiting to be shown to our table her husband posed one of the most honest and direct questions I had been asked in some time.

"Is it hard to be one of the only black people in town?" he asked. "For instance, how does it feel when you walk into the football stadium and there aren't any other black people there?" He noticed my hesitation in answering him.

"How do you like working for the district?" he added. He genuinely wanted to know. I was amazed at his directness, and I told him so.

"I appreciate the openness of the people in this town," I said. "I am also grateful that the district has been welcoming to me, since I am their first black superintendent. It's a completely different experience given my previous two superintendent positions."

My new friend listened intently.

"My first superintendent job in southern Wisconsin was in a racially diverse school district," I explained. "The second, in northern Chicago, was an almost entirely black community. This district is the exact opposite of both of those places."

My answer was honest but very diplomatic and guarded. I generally only discussed my true feelings and perceptions about race with people I knew and trusted so they wouldn't circulate throughout the community or appear in the local newspaper. (As you might imagine, writing a book on this subject is a great leap out of my comfort zone!)

After dinner I went back to my apartment and began to reflect more about the role of race in my life. This may sound strange, but I came to realize that race is my constant companion. It's not that people aren't friendly; it's just that I feel that I am always black first and Milt second.

When I was younger I hardly noticed it at all. I was idealistic, and I guess I didn't want to believe that racism had any power to limit what I could become. Although I'm confident in my leadership in my field of education, I continually stumble into awkward situations in my profession where I feel like an anomaly. In 2013 I attended an educator training conference in a suburb west of Milwaukee. Since it was in a remote place and the district vehicle I drove didn't have a navigation system like the one in my own car, I got lost and arrived about thirty minutes late.

I walked in the door, and as usual, I was the only black person at the event. Even though I saw a friend who was a former graduate instructor of mine, I still felt a stinging uneasiness. I tried to slip in unnoticed, embarrassed at being late. As I took off my overcoat my eyeglasses fell out of the pocket and rattled onto the floor. At the same time a box of mints tumbled out of another coat pocket, a few of them spilling out onto the floor. I was so embarrassed that I didn't pick them up. I then found a seat and took out my iPad and tried to hook up to the network so that I could participate in the training, but no matter how many times

I tried the password I could not get online. This meant that I required additional attention from a tech—the last thing I wanted—as that would only draw further attention to myself. All the while I felt completely stupid. At one point I was so frustrated that I almost got up and left.

I was having a theatrical inner moment! In my mind it seemed that everyone else's all-consuming focus was on me, but in reality probably nobody else really noticed. I was finally able to connect to the network, and later in the training when we switched to another Web site I was one of the first ones to be able to navigate it. I felt smart, but then I stopped to think about how I was feeling on the inside. I wondered why such a small circumstance caused me so much inner turmoil.

I know what you're thinking. If you were in similar circumstances you would be embarrassed as well. But I would ask you if you feel the additional weight of being a representative of your race. You see, I didn't want them to think that I was inferior in any way. My inability to connect to the network when everyone else could not only made me feel inferior; I was also concerned that it would reflect negatively on all future black people or black superintendents. This is part of what I call *the black man's burden*, the feeling that an individual black man represents the black race at all times and in every circumstance. *The black man's burden* manifests itself in other circumstances as well. If I go out to eat and there are some black people arguing or talking loudly I feel embarrassed, as if I am somehow responsible for and tied to their behavior. It's a feeling of guilt by association. It's bizarre, and it's not true, but it *is* how I feel in those situations. And I am not alone in this. I've talked with other middle class and professional black people who feel the same burden.

Certainly, this encumbrance is not limited to blacks. People in all kinds of minority or ethnic groups endure stereotypes, and "guilt by association" comes with the territory. Do you carry such a burden? Do you realize how stereotypes can provoke embarrassment or even a desire to deny one's identity in order to fit in? Even when they are positive, the pressure to live up to them can lead to frustration or even a sense of shame.

I've asked some of my white friends, "When you walk into an eating establishment and another white patron acts like a fool, do you feel any embarrassment or responsibility for that behavior, being a member of the same race?" They've told me, "No, of course not. I just keep eating." To quote Shakespeare, "There's the rub."

Normally I process a lot of my feelings about race with Peggy. She has been my best friend and confidante, but she has also been a sounding board and she keeps me centered. For years I thought I was going through my racial journey alone, but Peggy has helped me to see that she is having the same experience. People stare at her. They indict her character for marrying someone outside of her race. She has had to watch the effects of prejudice upon her husband and her sons. She feels what I feel.

There are times when I see things from a distorted perspective, and she reflects reality back to me. There are other times when I minimize the impact of race in a particular situation and she sets me straight. Peggy's ability to read people and situations has helped me through the years, and I've always had her unconditional love and support.

Chapter 2
THE SUPERFICIAL WOUND

A T THE RISK of over-generalizing, I wonder if most white people notice the unequal representation of races in society. The 2016 Academy Awards drew widespread criticism when, for the second year in a row, all the nominees for actors were white. A similar controversy surfaced surrounding the famous comedian Jerry Seinfeld following the 2014 Super Bowl, raising the question, "Why aren't any of the main characters of his sitcom black?" Mr. Seinfeld's response is germane: that people needed to "get a life," and he wondered why anyone would insert race into this topic. The point is that many white people are oblivious to the issue of race because they've always held a prominent place in our culture.

Hollywood is able to prick the consciences of people on the issue of racial injustice with movies like *The Butler* or *12 Years a Slave*, eliciting remorse and even tears, but the wound that these movies inflict on the conscience is not very deep if it doesn't produce real change. A scraped knee is more easily forgotten than an anguished heart, but these movies are more than entertainment. As you will see in further chapters, my own parents' stories—similar to those of many other blacks of their day—are not unlike scenes from popular films like *Driving Miss Daisy* and *The Help*, which artfully bring their characters to life.

Some white people feel a sense of responsibility for America's past injustices toward blacks. They believe that white privilege is a legitimate matter, and they admit that

11

they have profited in life simply from being white. Others do not. I recall a book that my high school English teacher had me read. *Farnham's Freehold*, by Robert A. Heinlein, is about a post-Apocalyptic world after a nuclear holocaust, which somehow gave black people the upper hand. The white people in the story were enslaved and made to suffer continuous indignities. They did not know how to react since their lives were regulated and restricted by rules and social conventions determined by the black people, who were now in control.

If being white does not posture people for success in life more than people of color, how would the following scenario play out? Let's say that God appeared to you in a vision and said that He wanted to give you the choice of being any race that you wanted to be in the United States. If you are white, and you can honestly say that you would choose to be black, then there is certainly no perceived benefit to being white. Even in the church, where racial and ethnic distinctions are to have no relevance, I think you would find very few takers. I believe if the Lord offered that choice to many blacks, though they would be ashamed to admit it, more than a few would choose to be white. It would not be a matter of black pride; it would hinge on their belief that life and opportunities would come much easier without the obstacles that race impose. Although white guilt is typically a negative motivator, I believe it can serve a purpose on an awareness level. First, it brings forth an acknowledgement by white people of past wrongs, even if only on a collective level. Second, it helps whites to think about people groups around them whom they might otherwise minimize or ignore. Slavery may be past history for whites, but it's part of the DNA of blacks, so acknowledgement of it is important in helping both blacks and whites legitimize the hurts that many of us still endure to this day.

If you talk to a Jewish person about their history it's clear that the Holocaust is woven into their DNA and identity. I knew a World War II veteran who referred to the Japanese in a very derogatory manner, though the war had long been over. In his generation, hatred of the Japanese was entrenched into their psyche because of the horrific attack on Pearl Harbor. What if the Japanese had publicly and formally apologized for Pearl Harbor after the war? What impact would that have had in helping this veteran forgive and move past that bitter memory? The Bible talks about the obligation of those who do wrong to come to their brother and confess the wrong that they have done. It also talks about the obligation of the offended party to forgive, even if the offense is repeated is clear in Scripture. (See Luke 17:4; Matthew 18:21–22.)

Being in education, I have sat in numerous diversity trainings where the concept of white privilege was addressed. My white friends and school administrators cringed anytime it was brought up. They hated being manipulated into feeling that they were somehow causatively involved in something that robbed blacks of opportunities. They also were offended because they believed strongly that their success was only attributable to their hard work and effort. I have had many discussions about this, and I can sympathize with their feelings.

I do not believe they contributed to a system that intentionally creates disadvantages for people of color. They are not part of a conspiracy. Whether or not they benefit from a system that has been in place for a long time in this country and still has residual effects, however, is left up to question.

I have attended numerous educator conferences in Wisconsin, including an annual gathering of about four hundred school district administrators from across the state. At the time of this writing only two of these district administrators are black, and one is Hispanic. Many times I am the only person of color at the conference.

Few people like to be in such situations; it's uncomfortable. Many times as I sat there feeling conspicuous I resolved to accept this as my lot since I chose to be a superintendent in this particular state. I've had no illusions of the racial representation changing significantly anytime soon, and I have wondered if anybody else at the conference noticed this lack of diversity and the impact it might be having on the student population.

For the first time since our nation was founded, whites are predicted to soon represent less than half of the population. According to the 2012 US Census Bureau, the population of the United States is 62.2 percent white, 17.4 percent Hispanic, 12.4 percent black, and 5.2 percent Asian.[1] But with the variations that are being created by biracial births it is much more complex than that. By the year 2050 a major shift is expected, so where are the role models for children of color? Why are leaders being selected who represent the demographics of the past rather than reflecting the reality of this change? White children also need exposure to adults of different races so they will be able to function in a world that is changing.

Over the years I've had numerous conversations with other black administrators who, like me, also aspired to become superintendents in Wisconsin. We came to the conclusion that it was not going to happen. Little did we realize that two of us would eventually have opportunities in communities with very few people of color.

I remember a conversation that I had with a friend. I called him because I was discouraged about the limited opportunities for blacks to land a job as a superintendent in the state of Wisconsin. "Have you applied for any of the superintendent positions that are open in the state?" I asked him.

"I have, and I am not really hopeful," he answered. "I know upper level administrators in Milwaukee Public Schools who have applied for various districts and could not even get an interview."

I told him that I'd applied to a suburban Milwaukee district and couldn't get an interview either. "You have been in some of the top districts in the state in various administrative positions," I said. "You have a pedigree. If you can't get a job, what hope do the rest of us have?"

He said he was going to apply for some jobs in Minnesota. "They seem to be more open," he said. "I don't believe a black man can get a job as a superintendent in most of this state."

To our surprise, he got a job as a superintendent in Wisconsin. It was in a district where he had held an administrative position before. I called him to congratulate him. "You must not be black anymore!" I joked.

A significant development arose during a 2014 conference. To my surprise, the state superintendent, Tony Evers, rose to his feet and began to talk about a task force he created to examine the issue of equity in education in Wisconsin—a state with one of the lowest graduation rates for black males at only 59.2 percent, compared to 93.6 percent for white males. He also said the average composite ACT score for black males was 16 as compared to 23 for whites.[2] He addressed the composition of the task force, and then he boldly went where very few dare to go.

In his comments he identified that the problem in the state of Wisconsin was a racial achievement gap. This was a very stunning acknowledgement.

I almost fell out of my chair! As an educator I have spent my career trying to close the achievement gap, using multiple strategies to help kids of color achieve better academic results. I have run traditional public schools as well as a charter school. I have used multiple levels of college prep curriculum. I have brought in people to prep students on the ACT test structure. I have done everything that I possibly could and have had limited success because the solution is not to be found exclusively in education.

I had participated in discussions over the course of my career as an administrator in the state, and no one was courageous enough to grab the bull by the horns. He went on to explain that if you compare the achievement of poor white children with the achievement of even affluent black children, the poor white children had higher achievement, as a group. If poverty was not the variable, he stated, it had to be race. When he concluded his remarks, he invited our questions.

I was so excited! I stood up and nervously said, "I want to commend you for having the courage to address this issue head on. Obviously, I am the only African-American superintendent in the room and wanted to tell you how excited I feel that you are willing to acknowledge this issue. I am a native Wisconsinite," I continued, "having grown up in Racine and being educated in the public schools there. I believe something has to be done to change the achievement of African-American males. If we do not succeed in closing this gap it will have negative economic effects on the entire state of Wisconsin." Afterward many people from the conference came to me and expressed their appreciation for what I had to say.

I have to applaud this recent development. It reinforces the fact that people of goodwill can change their thinking and rise up with courage to tackle the thorny problems and issues of their day. Now there are honest questions to grapple with as we face the issues head on. If poverty is not the culprit, exactly what is it about race that leads to the achievement gap? Are other factors related to the higher percentage of single-parent households in the black community responsible? What do scientific and environmental studies say about black–white differences? Have blacks rejected education and achievement as part of white culture? Have they lost the attitude of my parents' generation that compelled them to make sacrifices for the sake of the next generation? Have government policies led blacks to depend on government support rather than self-reliance? Are there residual impacts of racism that compound the attendant factor of poverty and retard the achievement of blacks?

I can think of no better segment of society to lead the way than the church. I am seeing a generation of Christians who are living out the implications of the gospel on race. You will see real diversity in some cutting-edge congregations, and it's not a matter of filling quotas. I recently watched a worship conference that was held at Charis Bible College in Colorado. The musical styles and the ethnicities of the presenters gave a glimpse of heaven. The music of worship draws people in; if it lacks rhythm or passion it will not draw a diverse audience. From what I can see this is changing. Churches that are supporting the adoption of African-American orphans are also making a large impact into society's hurts and wounds by the compassion of the Lord. Hallelujah!

Chapter 3
ARZELL AND MARY THOMPSON

WHEN THE MOVIE *Driving Miss Daisy* came out in 1989 my parents went to see it and talked about how much they liked it. I wondered how much of himself my father saw in Morgan Freeman's character, Hoke Colburn, who played the chauffeur for a wealthy southern white woman. Dad was kind and good-natured like Hoke, but their similarities didn't end there.

My mother, on the other hand, was stern and somewhat stoic, but her deep devotion to God and family brought out the best in us. Mom was born on April 14, 1912, the same night the *Titanic* sank. She always found the coincidental timing of her birth to that tragic event amusing.

My parents were not willing to settle for the way things were. They were the outliers in their families, always willing to embrace change. They were both from Northern Mississippi—my dad from the town of Okolona and my mom from outside a town called Houston.

It was always interesting to hear the differences between the father I knew as a child and the memories of my older brothers, as there is a ten-year gap between us. My father was still growing up when they were born and was beginning to be an adult when my younger brother Stan and I were born.

My parents grew up in the Jim Crow South. Jim Crow is the name for a collection of laws that completely governed the lives of black people in the South from the late 1800s until the 1960s. It was a straightjacket, constricting all opportunities for blacks, assuring that they would never live lives similar to whites. Jim Crow laws legislated what section of the bus a black person was allowed to sit in. Blacks could go to see a movie, but there were laws about where they could sit and what they could sit on within the theater. The law also confined blacks to drinking from separate water fountains and legislated separate bathrooms for "colored people."

Jim Crow was completely dehumanizing for blacks. In the history of the United States, Native Americans and blacks are the only groups that have faced such an overt and comprehensive attempt to hold them down by restricting all areas of their lives. The Supreme Court decision that upheld these laws was the *Plessy v. Ferguson*, which established the concept of "separate but equal." Most of the time, facilities were separate, but they were certainly not equal. This was especially true in educational institutions; *separate* meant "inferior" for blacks.

I want you, the reader, to think about what it would have been like to be either of my parents growing up in that world. I want you to understand the context of the world in which they lived and the limitations that were imposed upon them.

FLUKIE

My dad's name was Arzell Thompson Jr., and the only other people named Arzell that I knew growing up were members of my family. Dad was born on February 22, 1917, and his first job was working in a funeral home doing odd jobs, including transporting the bodies, assisting the morticians, and washing their cars. He was well liked, and people around town trusted him with their most prized possessions, paying him to wash and wax their cars. It was a job that he continued to do while my brothers and I were growing up. In fact, we would help him and get paid well for it. Dad was a generous man.

In the years that followed my dad's likeability and work ethic would lead to a long stint as a chauffeur. When he and my mother settled in Missouri in the 1940s he worked for Mr. Harris, a wealthy, white gentleman who owned Harris Lumberyard.

My father often told me stories of driving all around the United States. He told me of driving up Pike's Peak on perilous mountain roads. He also told me about accompanying Mr. Harris to exotic places like Key West, Florida, and Havana, Cuba. My father would drive Mr. Harris to New York, where he visited the Cotton Club, a famous entertainment hot spot in Harlem. He listened to the now-legendary entertainers who performed there, including Louis Armstrong, Cab Calloway, and Duke Ellington, to name a few. My dad saw a lot of interesting things when he traveled with Mr. Harris.

There were other things that I would learn about my father that were remnants of his chauffeuring days. He was in his seventies when I discovered, at a wedding, that my dad was quite a good dancer. He could really do the jitterbug! When Peggy's sister got married, my parents attended the wedding since they were close friends of my in-laws. When the band started to play some rock and roll music, Dad got up and asked Peggy's Aunt Ethel to dance. They were jiving and doing all of those affectations that you only see on *Dancing With the Stars*. I loved it so much that I have since learned to jitterbug. I'm not anywhere near the dancer that my father was, but I'm still learning.

I never heard Dad recall any memory in which Mr.

Harris mistreated him. This, however, did not insulate him from the attitudes and treatment of black people during those times. During his years as a chauffeur my dad would suffer the indignities that all black people in the South endured, eating behind diners and restaurants while his boss ate inside, not being allowed to stay in the same hotel as his boss, or even eating at the same lunch counters as white people.

Although I knew the background of my mother's faith, I didn't know much about my father's. When I think back to the times we visited his parents in Mississippi I don't recall attending church with them. I do know, however, that my father was influenced by my mother's faith, and he attended weekly church services with her. When he received Christ after I shared my testimony with him when I was twenty-one, it was part of a decades-long process of his journey of faith.

My dad didn't have a formal education. Why would he go to elementary or to high school during those times? What opportunities would education open for a black man in the South? Sure, there were black doctors and teachers, but these highly educated men were impacted by the same segregation and restrictive laws as were those who were uneducated. They practiced medicine in segregated hospitals, which served black patients, or in courthouses representing black clients, but how did their education provide an escape from the discrimination that surrounded them? Preparing for college would have been as realistic for my father as planning to go to the moon. As a result he had about a third-grade education.

I never realized how ashamed my father was of the fact that he misspoke certain words and needed my mom to read most of their documents and bills over the years. She handled the family's finances, and I thought nothing of it because he covered it over with his gregarious personality and his ability to tell amazing stories. I didn't find out how much his lack of education bothered him until I was a teenager.

Dad must have been in his fifties when I went into his bedroom looking for something (with his permission). When I opened his top dresser drawer I found an unlikely collection of children's books, like the *Ugly Duckling* and *The Little Red Hen*. It then hit me that my dad didn't know how to read! I felt badly for him, but I never brought the subject up, even though I would later become an educator. It would have shamed him. After this experience I understood why he encouraged my brothers and me to get as much education as possible. Ultimately, two of us earned master's degrees. I can still remember the picture of Stan wearing his crimson robe at his graduation from Harvard University. Dad was standing beside him, and it was hard to tell who was prouder in that picture.

Despite his lack of education and heavy southern accent Dad was one of the most outgoing people I have ever known. People took an immediate liking to him, and when he died in 2002 there were people at his funeral who had known him the entire fifty years he'd lived in Racine. He loved to talk with people, and no one was a stranger to him. As kids that drove us crazy when we went out to Dairy Queen in our neighborhood. Still holding our treats, he would strike up a conversation with a stranger while our ice cream cones turned soggy and our banana splits became soup. This friendliness was never more evident than when we took a trip together when I was twenty-five years old.

In 1977 Peggy and I had accepted jobs at Sterling

College, and my parents volunteered to help us make the move to Sterling, Kansas. Whenever we stopped along the way, I noticed that even though my dad was a big black man, six feet four inches tall and about two hundred and fifteen pounds, people were immediately comfortable with him. At a McDonald's an elderly lady began talking to him as if he had been a lifelong friend. He projected an image of acceptance toward others and seemed to always get acceptance in return. He disarmed people with his affable persona.

His friends nicknamed him Flukie when he was a youngster, the origins of which he could never explain to me. This nickname became his real name to a lot of people. When he passed in 2002 some of his lifelong friends didn't recognize the name "Arzell Thompson" in the newspaper obituary. They didn't even know who this Arzell Thompson was. When I was growing up people would ask me who my daddy was, and if I answered, "Arzell Thompson," they would look at me quizzically. I would see their confusion and mention "Flukie," and then they would smile and tell me that I looked a little bit like him.

In time I would find out that knowing people only by their nicknames was not uncommon either for my dad's family or his roots. Since my dad was an only child, his aunts and cousins were like sisters to him. They had played together and fought together. I was in my forties when I met his aunt during one of my visits to the South during the late nineties. Her nickname was Peter Rabbit. I laughed when I heard it because I'd never met anyone who was nicknamed after a fictional character! Curious, I later asked Dad what his aunt's real name was. He thought about it for the longest time, but all he could produce was a blank stare. Even my mother mused about it, and it took her a day or two before she figured out that Peter Rabbit's real name was Edna.

MARY ALICE

As with most married couples, my parents' personalities were very different, partly a result of their contrasting childhood backgrounds. Dad was an open book who wore his feelings on his sleeves. He didn't carry offenses long but would let you know if his feelings were hurt. Mom, on the other hand, played it close to the vest. If she was offended at you, her feelings were a lot more nuanced. She hid them, and figuring her out was like reading a deep mystery.

Mary Alice was the eldest of fourteen children. She grew up on a farm and had to mediate between her younger siblings and help raise them. Given the times and what I remember, my grandparents might have been sharecroppers.

In contrast, Dad grew up in town, the son of a railroad worker, living in the lap of luxury (for a southern black child). His people were not rich, but they were what black people called "good livers." Mom grew up poor, however. Some of her siblings died young of diseases and medical conditions like epilepsy. Health care was not available for blacks unless they traveled to the black hospital in town.

I was named after my mother's father, Milton Barr. He was a gentle man. I don't remember a coarse word ever coming out of his mouth when I was a child. I respected my grandfather, but I feared my maternal grandmother. Lela was a little different. If you misbehaved she could whip your behind with a switch! Though my grand- mother was a little more volatile than my grandfather in temperament, my mother would tell me that she never heard a cross word between her parents.

Mom shared some of her family background with me. Her parents were light skinned, and I knew that we had mixed ancestry. Mom's grandmother was of German descent. When you think of the period between 1860 and 1900, when her grandmother would have given birth to a black child, you cannot even imagine the treatment she endured. Although my mother didn't talk a lot about it, I wish I had been more curious about it when I was younger. The stories would have been fascinating. The German heritage of my mother played itself out in the fact that she didn't get highly emotional about things. The only occasions that come to mind would be when she was listening to Mahalia Jackson or singing a hymn around the house. Then the tears would flow.

Like her parents, she was not a yeller. She didn't have to yell. Though she was no taller than five feet four inches, we all listened to her. We knew that she loved us, and she would demonstrate it to us both in love and discipline. Once when Stan and I were jumping on Mom and Dad's bed, we jumped so hard it broke. We stopped and looked at each other with wide eyes knowing what was to follow. When Mom came up the stairs you could see how mad she was. She went outside and got a switch. In the vernacular, it was a nice "keen" switch; this meant that it had flexibility but not breakability. My brother proudly announced that he was not going to run away but "take it like a man." True to his word, he stood there and took a few swipes from the switch. I, however, was not going to take it like a man. I was going to take the coward's way out and try to outrun her! Though by that time I was a little taller than my short mother, and my knees were pumping and my arms were flailing, she used her little, short legs and caught up to me and gave me more than my brother got. I recall this memory with laughter now because I know that she did it out of love, but that day it didn't seem so loving. You can tell from this story that my mother was raised old-school as far as child-rearing. This also meant that if a baby was crying in her family she would not just pick the child up or coo with it. Babies were only picked up if they were wet or hungry.

Mary Alice's first job as an adult was working in a hospital, cooking and doing the laundry. She never talked about it, but she had been married before she met my father. Her first husband was a drinker, and although the marriage did not last long my elder brothers, Lewis and Linton, were from that marriage.

Some time after her divorce she was introduced to a tall, likable young man from town. Arzell was five years younger than my mother, and she said he seemed to be spoiled, being an only child. Somehow, though, all of this endeared him to her.

My mother was educated, having graduated from high school—a real accomplishment back then. She wanted to go to college, but several things played against her. She was black. She was a woman. And worst of all, she was in the south in the 1930s. She might have been able to attend a black college, but even with a college education, what real opportunity was there to excel in the South? Her father did not support her aspirations and would not let her pursue her education.

Eventually she moved to Kinloch, Missouri, to take a domestic job, cleaning and cooking for the Polks, a wealthy white family, where she was also able to raise Lewis and Linton. Arzell wasn't about to let a good woman go, so he began asking around to find out where she went. When he caught up with her they began dating, and after they married they lived on the Polk property, where Dad found a job working as a chauffeur for Mr. Harris.

If the early scenes of my dad's life seemed to jump out of the movie *Driving Miss Daisy*, my mom's path was not unlike the black women in the 2011 film *The Help*. She would cook, clean, and do laundry for the Polks. My brother Jim remembers the home they lived in on the Polk property as little more than a shack.

There have been many times when I've compared my mother's life to that of my father-in-law, Charles Might. They both grew up on farms. They were both very bright people. One grew up in Mississippi, the other in northwestern Ohio. While my mother worked most of her life as a domestic and also catered dinner parties for the wealthy, my father-in-law went to college and received his bachelor's and master's degrees from Ohio State University. What might have happened if my mother had the same opportunities as Charles? Would her exceptionality have been recognized, had she been given the chance to spread her wings and fly? We will never know.

My most prevalent memory of my mother is of her sitting with a book in her lap. She read all the time. Much of the time it was the Bible, but she also read works of literature, magazines, and other genres. She had such a love of learning that any time an encyclopedia salesman came to the door she was an easy mark. She was frugal in almost everything else, but not when it came to books for her children. She did anything that she could to provide opportunities for us to grow intellectually. Perhaps she wanted to live out her own dreams through us.

I will never forget the day that my parents drove me

to college in western Wisconsin. The four-hour trip was very beautiful as we drove through rolling hills and bluffs. I never asked them if they had ever been in that part of the state. I was so excited; I just wanted to get there. I was oblivious to the excitement that my parents felt as they walked around the campus at the University of Wisconsin–La Crosse. They wanted to linger, soaking it all in, but selfishly I just wanted them to get in the car and leave so I could get on with college life. As I look back, I should have been more aware of the gravity of that moment and the fact that this was a high point in *their* lives too. This moment was the fulfillment of their own dream and a culmination of the drive that they had to create a better life for us all.

Back when my parents first moved to Racine, my mother cleaned the homes of doctors and high-level business people, some of them among the most prominent people in town. She was also an exceptional cook. After making the gourmet dishes that their dinner parties required she would then come home and make black-eyed peas and cornbread for us. From time to time though, she would show off her cooking acumen for us as well. She made each member of the family's favorite pastry. My dad loved pineapple upside-down cake. Junior loved sweet potato pie. Stan loved apple pie, and Jim loved pumpkin pie. Although she died in 2001, one of my greatest hopes is that when I get to heaven Jesus will allow her to have a cherry pie waiting for me in her oven when I arrive there!

Outside of her job Mom was a leader. She was involved in activities like the women's society at St. John's Methodist Church. This leadership role was never more evident than in a story that my brother Arzell told me after mom had passed about how she helped him to get his job at Twin

Disc as a technical illustrator. Mom was not one to mince words. She talked with John Batten, the president of Twin Disc, and asked him why there weren't any blacks in management positions in his manufacturing company. She also mentioned that she had a son who had just finished an eight-year stint in the air force and had been trained as a technical illustrator who was looking for a job. A few weeks later my brother got a call from Twin Disc. He interviewed and got the job.

Unlike my father, my mother had no need to be self-conscious about her education. She spoke proper English, and because she was well read and had a broad vocabulary she could move in a variety of social circles. She developed friendships with different types of people, exposing our family to people outside the circle of our working class.

One of her friends, Madonna Martens, lived in an upper-middle-class neighborhood in the outskirts of Racine. At that time in the 1960s I do not recall any black people living in that area of town. Prior to visiting their house with my parents for dinner I had never been in a house with a finished basement, a family room, and a fireplace. At the time I thought only rich people could afford these things. In the years since I have come to realize that they were only middle class. The Martens' son, Chris, was my age, so I had someone to play with. They were great people, and I liked them a lot, yet I came to believe that there were very few people more exceptional than my own parents, who simply didn't have the same opportunities to prosper because of their race. This would be a continual theme that played out their lives. They were good, well-liked, hard-working people with great social skills. They only lacked the one ingredient at that time to give them a chance at success in America: being white.

Chapter 4
FOLLOW THE NORTH STAR

I GREW UP AROUND people who had immigrated to the United States from other countries to pursue a better life. They chose to leave their families and all that was familiar to them, believing they would encounter new opportunities and a new mind-set. Most blacks, however, did not come to this country by choice. They were literally dragged here as slaves, and for the most part they remained as such in a culture that was rooted in slavery. Even post-slavery, the culture promulgated the separation of the races. From the nineteenth century well into the twentieth century, southern culture continued to foster repression with cross-burnings and lynchings, clearly indicating that blacks may no longer have been slaves, but they were also not yet truly free.

It is not lost on me that there have been several significant migrations northward that have impacted the lives of black people. The Underground Railroad, which helped slaves escape north, was the first. It did not affect as many black people as you might think, however. Perhaps thousands escaped north, but given the fact that there were several million slaves in America, it did not have a significant impact on the masses, other than the hope it kindled.

The second significant northward move of blacks came in two waves. Some relocated north following World War I. My parents were part of the second wave of the Great Migration of blacks during the years 1940–1970 when five million people, fed up with life in the South, headed north and west. I wonder if that population was drawn by the same dynamics that gave hope and opportunity to immigrants.

Although their roots were in Mississippi, no decision that my parents made had a greater impact on our family than moving to Wisconsin. I have tried to imagine what my life would have been like if they had remained in the South. Given the era in which I grew up, nothing would have been the same.

In the 1940s when my parents were beginning raise their family the South was a crippling place to live. The prospects for a life of fulfillment were not available to black people. It was a white world, and there were no signs that it was going to change any time soon.

They first moved from Mississippi to St. Louis, but it wasn't much better there. St. Louis was still the South, though the form of prejudice was *Jim Crow lite* compared to the Deep South. My parents eventually saw the writing on the wall. It was understood that there were certain jobs that blacks could not have and sections of town they could not live in.

My mother had a brother, James, who had made the move north several years earlier. He left to work for American Motors in Kenosha, Wisconsin, where he bought a house in nearby Racine and commuted the ten miles to work. Uncle James loved to fish, so living along Lake Michigan was a perfect fit. American Motors did not operate year round. It had an uneven work schedule, and there would be times where the plant would shut down for weeks at a time, but Uncle James didn't mind. In fact, he welcomed them as a signal to go fishing.

The standard of living for blacks in the Racine/Kenosha area was one of the highest in the nation at the time. There was an abundance of factories with jobs that paid a good wage. Though they couldn't buy a house in certain neighborhoods due to the unwritten rules of discrimination about selling to blacks, there were still a lot more choices and opportunities than blacks were experiencing in the South. And my uncle was a good salesman, promoting to his relatives the prosperity that he enjoyed while living in Wisconsin.

As a risk-taker, my father didn't mind new experiences. He wanted to make something of his life, and he cared about opportunities for his children. As I think back, that was one of the characteristics that separated my mother and father from some of their siblings; my parents were pioneers.

When my Uncle James shared the opportunities available to my father, Dad was all in. He traveled north for a visit, and he saw that there were jobs. He considered working for American Motors like his brother-in-law, but the frequent shutdowns of the plant were of real concern to him. With a young family, he needed steady income. My half-brothers, Lewis and Linton, remained in the South with their father, Harvey, but Mom and Dad had two younger sons, James, age ten, and Arzell Jr., age eight, to support.

Although Racine had other places to work like J I Case, Massey-Ferguson, and Twin Disc, to name just a few, my dad was uneducated. While this would not have impaired the limited opportunities for blacks in the South since most jobs were unskilled, it did close some doors in the North. This led to Dad's choice to work in a foundry in Racine. Belle City, aka Racine Steel Casting, made large parts for Caterpillar Machinery.

Dad moved first and then sent for the family. When my

mom and brothers joined him in Racine in 1950 it was an interesting town to live in. Blacks were moving there in significant numbers from Mississippi, Alabama, and Tennessee, to name just a few southern states. Growing up in Racine, it was amazing to me how many people my parents knew who had migrated. They were either from the same general area as my parents, or they had common friends or relatives in the South. It was like Facebook without the Internet. Over time, my brothers Lewis and Linton also moved to Racine.

The ethnic diversity was very interesting. There were people moving to Racine from Mexico, Yugoslavia, Turkey, Greece, Italy, Armenia, Russia, Poland, and Czechoslovakia. They joined the German and Danish immigrants of a previous generation who had already established themselves and their fine bakeries in the city. Many of these people lived together in the same neighborhoods. There was not the same kind of racial segregation that separated people intentionally and residentially as there had been in the South.

I am not saying that all of these new immigrants melted into one society. They didn't necessarily worship or socialize together, but they mowed their lawns next door to each other and sent their children to the same schools. They also looked out for each other. I knew that I couldn't create mischief in my neighborhood! I was accountable to all of my neighbors, no matter what their ethnic and racial background was. I knew I had to be on my best behavior. If my friends and I did something wrong they would shake their fingers at us, and worse yet, they would tell on us to our parents. They knew us!

When I was a teenager my father made me the snow thrower for some of the widows and elderly single people in the neighborhood. No, I didn't throw snow at them; I had to shovel their walks since they had no one else to help them. I hated doing this because they only paid me with a few quarters after I removed a foot or more of snow from their incredibly long sidewalks and driveways. I would complain about it to my father, but he didn't care. He felt a sense of responsibility for those ladies who didn't have husbands and children to take care of them.

As I look back now I know why people respected my dad: he was a good neighbor. Some showed their appreciation for this by attending his funeral when he died decades later.

Chapter 5
AGE OF DISCOVERY

I WAS ONE OF four boys in the Thompson household. James and Junior were there to greet me when I was born. In 1957 my brother Stan came along. Dad and mom had worked hard, and by the time I was five years old they bought their first house on the north side of Racine, on St. Patrick Street.

The screened-in porch on our two-story home gave us an opportunity to sit outside late into the night. I fondly remember one night when our whole family slept on the porch just for fun. We had a large backyard, and our neighbors were people in the same stage of life, mostly young families starting out.

Due to the fact that many people from different countries and ethnicities settle there, Racine was a gathering place for the trappings of many different cultures. This was especially true where food was concerned. When I visited our neighbors, their inviting homes smelled of German, Eastern European, and Hispanic cuisine. Mr. Byrd lived next door. The Eisels lived across the street; they were German. In time the Villareals would move into the neighborhood from Mexico. We ate food from a Danish bakery down the street and became fond of pizza from DeRango's Italian restaurant.

My dad was the king of ethnic food. When I came home after school I never knew what zesty aromas I might be greeted with in the kitchen. Would it be sauerkraut and Polish sausages with a chaser of hog's head cheese?

Would it be Mexican food topped off with some sauce that a coworker dared him to eat because it was so hot that it was nuclear? Or would it be some other strange foreign delicacy? My palate lived in a constant state of wonder and surprise.

Although my neighborhood was diverse my earliest memory of race and being different occurred in kindergarten. It was also my first amorous encounter. I thought Debbie, a little girl in my class, was the most beautiful creature on Earth! She was friendly, and I thought her curly brown hair was so cute. We used to hold hands, and then at recess one day I kissed her. It was an impulsive act born of puppy love and innocence. I don't think she minded; we were just mimicking what we saw older people do.

But later that day the teacher brought me into the room. "What were you doing?" she sternly asked. Before I could answer she asked, "What were you thinking?"

"What do you mean?" I asked, confused.

"Why did you kiss Debbie?" she asked.

I was stymied. Why ask a child that question? Who knows what motivates a kindergartener to do anything? She just seemed so upset about it.

I was taken to the office. My parents were told about it, and I was warned that it was never to happen again. Later I would find out the reason why: Debbie was white. As for Debbie, she didn't react much. Race doesn't play a big part in the life of a kindergartener; that is, until adults instill a focus on what makes people different as opposed to what makes us similar. My five-year-old companions and I were not aware of the taboos of adult society. All we cared about was nap time, cookies, and milk. Debbie was a beautiful princess in my eyes—not a white princess. The over-the-top reaction of adults made me wonder what was wrong with me.

A few years later I had another distressing experience. Like most kids, my brother Stan and I loved Hostess Twinkies, cupcakes, and fruit pies; they were like mother's milk to us, so we walked up the street to the A&P grocery store. Walking through the door, we took just a few steps when we noticed a little boy—probably no older than four years old—sitting in a shopping cart staring intently at us. He was sizing us up. And then he turned to his mother and very matter-of-factly said, "Look mom, niggers!" I don't remember if Stan and I were angry with this or just shocked. It was completely unexpected. The word *nigger* was not freely thrown around in our world, and to hear it from such a young child was a surprise. Exchanging glances, my brother and I read each other's minds, as we were both thinking, "Who is this pipsqueak to call us anything?"

Growing up, I also became conscious of being different through the literature that I read. My mother, who was book-smart and had a naturally inquisitive mind, was a role model for me in this regard. I guess I admired that and tried to emulate her. She encouraged me to read the stories of people like George Washington Carver, the scientist who invented hundreds of uses for the peanut. I read the stories of Frederick Douglass and Harriet Tubman. Through this historic literature I developed a cadre of historical heroes.

It helped that I loved school. School was a refuge for me and reinforced a feeling of being smart. It also made me forget about my physical infirmities, which limited my life. Although I was later healed, thank the Lord, I had epilepsy and asthma when I was a young child, which made me feel both different and fragile. I loved sports but couldn't play them at that time. While my friends were dreaming of becoming major league baseball players or playing in the NFL I was imagining myself as a lawyer, an astronomer, or a nuclear physicist. I began to gain enough confidence that I competed with other students for academic recognition.

George Chardukian was one of the smartest kids I grew up with, and I wanted to be his equal. George was also a spectacular athlete, which became evident even in elementary school, but I knew I couldn't compete with him in that regard. George even tried to teach me how to hit a fastball. Talk about an exercise in futility!

I also knew what it was like to be one of the last kids picked for kickball or baseball. I was tall and skinny, and not being athletic, I stuck out like a sore thumb. Still, George was one of my best friends in elementary school, and we competed on spelling and other tests to see who could get higher grades. Whenever I won it was a shot in the arm. Two of my favorite instructors, John Hacarian and Lewelyn Williams, will never know how much their encouragement and excellent teaching laid the foundation upon which I am still building to this day.

The civil rights movement was unfolding from the time when I was born until about my fifteenth year. I watched history in the making as events in the South were being televised on the news. I remember seeing marches with peaceful demonstrators walking together and singing. There was footage of police dogs attacking people who were peacefully and quietly protesting their mistreatment. Just as graphic were images of police officers and firemen as they turned fire hoses on people who only wanted the right to vote or to be treated equally. I watched in horror as people were literally being washed down the street. I wondered how this squared with the ideals that I was being taught in school. I had read about the Thirteenth, Fourteenth, and Fifteenth Amendments of the Constitution and wondered how this kind of racism could be justified.

I was privileged enough to actually watch the news broadcast of Dr. Martin Luther King Jr.'s "I Have A Dream" speech. Of all the speeches in American history I believe there are two that are timeless and unique, speeches that people will recall from one generation to another. This is one of them. The "Gettysburg Address" is the other. As I watched his speech on television it just reinforced to me, even as a young child, that Dr. Martin Luther King Jr. represented a type of courage and inspiration that was worth emulating. He represented a life that transcended race and hatred.

These heroes gave me a sense of pride in the type of people that I came from, but to reconcile this with real life was difficult. The talk of brotherhood that sprang up in the sixties didn't jive with reality. I especially noticed that when I went to church. At school my friends were Irish, Danish, Polish, etc., but at church I was only with black people. We sang a lot of hymns and spirituals, music that found its origins in slavery. In past generations these songs about how Moses led the people of Israel out of captivity were sung as a means of hope that someday black people would similarly be free. In church they represented the same hopes and aspirations unrealized while black people were being mistreated, especially in the South.

As I have stated earlier, most of the kids I went to school with were the children of immigrants, and no one was exempt from bullying and jokes about their particular ethnicity. You might think this would have created a kind of brotherhood of suffering, but it was not so. My teenage memories drove home the fact that race was like a shadow, something I could not escape. I was in eighth grade when I had an experience that reinforced to me that I was an "other."

I went to Douglas Park after school with a bunch of guys whom I considered friends. We were in classes together at Washington Jr. High School, and most of us lived within a mile or so of one another. By this time I no longer had epilepsy or asthma, and I loved to play football with them. Some of our friends played basketball inside the community center, but we were diehards, playing football outside all the time into the coolness of the night. At this city park we tuned out the noisy traffic sounds, but we had to be careful not to punt the ball too far or it would go into the busy street. We always looked forward to getting a hamburger at the Circle K across the street after our games.

On that warm fall day we were laughing and joking and screaming over our spectacular plays, as we always did. At one point one of the guys fumbled the ball, and we all instinctively jumped on it. One of the guys stood by, watching the rest of us scramble for the loose ball and then pile on top of each other, and he shouted, "Nigger pile!" I looked at him and could tell that he felt embarrassed. It was a term that the guys would have used in private, without a black classmate there. Another friend, Joe, came up to me immediately and apologized, but the damage had been done. I would play with those guys again and go to classes with them all the way through high school graduation, but it would never be the same. That phrase told me that I would always be an outsider.

Trust lost is hard to regain. I don't remember going out for burgers with them after that.

Years have passed, and from time to time I still see some of those guys. Sometimes I get to play golf with them. I consider them friends, but that memory is still there. I've had to work through some of these memories, and I've chosen to forgive, but forgiveness can be very hard to perform. I say *perform* because it begins with a choice, an act of the will, and it's a commitment to follow through, but true forgiveness takes the grace of God.

It's difficult because the offense is often unjust and unrighteous, and it's real. Whether we feel slighted or misrepresented, snubbed or misunderstood, stabbed or misjudged, we are wounded in some way, and our emotions, if left unchecked, will quickly lead to bitterness. But if we choose to forgive instead of justifying our bitterness we can begin the process of letting go and moving on.

Forgiveness is divine; we forgive because Jesus Christ forgives us. Don't underestimate the power that God's Word has in affecting this change. The apostle Paul admonishes the church: "Therefore, as God's chosen people, holy and dearly loved, clothe yourselves with compassion, kindness, humility, gentleness and patience. Bear with each other and forgive one another if any of you has a grievance against someone. Forgive as the Lord forgave you. And over all these virtues put on love, which binds them all together in perfect unity" (Col. 3:12–14, NIV).

To forgive the way that God forgives means that you can also "forget" the hurt. You may never lose the memories of them—it's not always safe to do so—but only He can cause them to diminish and become ineffectual over time. He can take away the desire to rehearse the hurt over and over again, which perpetuates the cycle of hatred.

My parents modeled true forgiveness for me. They made the choice that they would not return evil for evil but good for evil, as Paul writes in Romans 12. Though they had suffered indignities while growing up, they refused to carry a lot of baggage from their years in the segregated South. They practiced what Jesus taught about forgiving those who despitefully use you and impressed me with the kind of faith that walked through the really difficult challenges in life.

Chapter 6
CROSSING THE LINE

THE HUMMING ENGINE and the hissing windows lulled me to sleep on the front bench seat of our old car as I was sandwiched between my dad and my brother. I became a human bobble head until I was jarred awake by the uncontrollable laughter of my brothers.

"What happened?" I asked, as I wiped the spittle off my chin.

"Your head was sort of floating and bobbing up and down while you were sleeping," they roared.

When we were kids our family often traveled south to visit our relatives. On many occasions, because of his chauffeur background, my dad would be a "real man" and drive straight through from Wisconsin to Mississippi, which was probably a fifteen-hour drive in those days due to road conditions and older cars. In northern Illinois we might even stop at Henri's, a fast food favorite of my dad's, where we'd order red hot dogs. I had never seen a hot dog with bright red casing before, and I thought their French fries and malts were spectacular.

On the trip, after reaching Cairo, Illinois, stopping for food or anything else was not an option, so my mother would pack provisions of sandwiches and a thermos full of lemonade. Sometimes we would carry a "pee pot" in the car, and if we had to go we used that. Other times my dad would pull over to the side of the road, and we would walk out into a field and do our business. For some reason I thought this procedure was normal when traveling, and it wasn't until a few years later that I realized why we never stopped. My parents didn't want to deal with the discrimination. We couldn't have eaten in the restaurants, and staying in a hotel was out of the question. My brothers and I learned to sleep in the car, which made the drive easier on our parents.

Sometimes along the way to Mississippi the first leg of our journey would take us to the inner city of St. Louis, where my mother's parents had relocated. They lived in a brownstone with my Uncle Steve and Aunt Ailene around the corner from a White Castle hamburger joint. Across the street was a huge city park where we always dashed off to play. Most of my cousins were my age, so it was the best of times.

We'd play hide-and-go-seek, cops and robbers, and all the usual childhood games. I especially liked playing with my cousins, Carl and Essie May, who were both funny and talented. Essie May liked to read like I did, and Carl played the piano by ear. These memories fill me with joy to this day. But another memory stuck in my mind, one that I didn't understand at the time. I noticed there were no white people to be seen in their neighborhood, which encompassed many square miles. I began to realize that the phrase *separate but equal* was not a choice but a mandate requiring blacks to live in different neighborhoods, attend different schools, and at times, shop in different stores.

After a few days it would be time to venture further south. At the time I didn't realize how much racism affected something as simple as traveling. My parents did their best to brief us about the proper protocol when we headed toward Mississippi. They told us that we had to say, "yes, sir" and "no, sir" and "yes, ma'am" and "no, ma'am" when addressing all people, especially whites. They also told us that when we bought something in a store in my dad's hometown of Okolona we would have to gently place the money on the counter and not carelessly slap it down, as we might have done in the North.

But they didn't tell us everything. Since they were used to the bowing and scraping that you had to do in the South they forgot that we were northerners in mind and soul, and we had a completely different orientation. They had grown up in a state where people were lynched for disrespecting white people and were abused if they tried to vote. They forgot to tell us that just being ourselves would be considered being "uppity."

My brother Jim had a frightening encounter in the 1950s when he was about thirteen years old. Being very young, I hadn't gone along on that trip. While visiting our relatives, Jim and Junior decided to go to a movie theater. They sat on fruit crates up in the balcony in the "colored" section, the only place black people were allowed in Mississippi movie theaters. Although they were born in the South, Jim and Junior became northerners in 1950, and the longer they lived in Racine the more "uppity" they appeared. It was about to get Jim into trouble.

Leaving the balcony of the theater, Jim went to the concession stand, where he walked up to the man behind the counter. "I would like a box of Good & Plenty," he said.

The man's eyes narrowed, and he leaned over the counter. "You would like some Good & Plenty *what*?" he demanded.

Jim was confused, not realizing the slight he had given to the southern white man. As the tension grew thick, a black onlooker realized that this was a serious situation. They were still lynching blacks in Mississippi in the late fifties. The man ran out of the theater and went to get my father.

"Flukie," he said, "you better run down to the movie theater. Something is going on with your son." My dad frantically ran to the theater, and when he arrived he gathered all of his social skills.

"That boy did not say 'sir' to me!" the man behind the counter huffed.

"I apologize for my son," my father said, his eyes asking for mercy. "He doesn't know better. He was raised in the North."

"You better teach him some respect, boy," retorted the man, who was younger than my father. My dad humbled himself to protect Jim, but it was a stance he knew all too well.

Our family vacations not only opened my eyes to racial discrimination, they also awakened me to poverty. I thought I was poor compared to some of my school friends until I saw real poverty in the South.

My relatives lived so far back in the woods that if we went to see them at night I was afraid something would jump out from behind a tree and just swallow me up! They lived in an old house that looked like it was put together with old planks of wood. It had a corrugated tin roof and, of course, no air-conditioning to deal with the searing summer heat. Winters do get cold in Mississippi, but one of my uncles didn't even have a furnace in his house until at least the 1970s. Sometimes we would visit them at Thanksgiving time when it was relatively warm during the day, but at night to keep warm we slept under more quilts than you'd find at an Amish quilting bee. The fireplace was in the next room, and only our noses stuck out from under the covers as we slept. Even my northern hide wasn't meant for that kind of cold.

Going to the bathroom at night was also a challenge. There was no indoor plumbing, so I learned not to eat or drink much in the evenings. If we had to go to the bathroom we took the flashlight or lantern, turned right at the cow pen, and looked for the little outhouse. There the toilet paper was not Cottonelle or White Cloud; there was a corncob or some cornhusks readily available. This was unacceptable to me. I was genteel compared to my cousins, so although it was a sure lesson in self-control, as I look back I think I must have developed bladder or kidney damage from having to hold it all night. I found that there were a variety of ways to suffer in the South.

I felt sorry for my cousins in Mississippi. I once visited their junior high school, and while I was happy to see the same history textbook that we used in my school, that's where the similarities ended. During the entire class they covered just one paragraph. One paragraph! We were in the same grade, but we would have covered half of the chapter at my school. The expectations and the amount of rigor were so low that I was embarrassed for my cousins. It was the fruit of *separate-but-equal* education.

After we left that history class we went to the gym, where they were playing music on a record player for a good part of the rest of the day. I kept waiting for the principal or someone to say that it was time to go to the next class and learn something. It didn't happen.

My cousins suffered when they grew up, and they continued to live in comparative poverty. Some have argued that the effects of racism ended in the past, but it had long-term effects upon my cousins' lives. To this day, many southern schools continue to fall below national norms while the relationship between poverty and racism continues to be debated.

Life was not perfect for us in the North, but I realized that my brothers and I enjoyed opportunities that would have been unavailable to us in the South. My last trip to Mississippi as a teenager happened when I was thirteen years old. My mom and my brother Stan were already there, and my dad and I were driving south. We had to stop for gas when we crossed into Mississippi, and I can vividly remember that as my dad filled the car I went in to go to the bathroom. This was 1966, and I didn't know that blacks and whites had separate bathrooms. My parents didn't prompt me on this because we normally didn't stop for gas in Mississippi. Being ignorant, I went into the bathroom nearest to the door and thought nothing of it. When I exited the service station I looked at my father. He was as white as a sheet! He could tell that I'd misunderstood and pointed out that I should have gone into the "colored" bathroom. He was genuinely afraid for both of our lives.

I loved my father and respected him, but I looked him right in the eye and spoke slowly and forcefully. "I am never going to go south with you again as long as I live," I told him. I was tired of having to treat southerners with deference just because they were white and we were black. "The next time you go, let me stay home with Lewis," I proposed. "He and Heddy can take care of me." Lewis was in his thirties and lived down the street, and his oldest kids were my age. My dad agreed, and I did not travel south with my parents again until the late 1990s when one of my mother's brothers passed away. By that time the South had changed; blacks owned businesses and were in management positions, but the damage from my childhood experience had already been done. To this day that memory still is painful.

Some people believe discrimination and prejudice are only things you read about in a history book, but these experiences are a part of my family's pathos. Today there are political commentators who question how long it will be before we no longer have to take into account the history of black Americans. Slavery was generations ago, they say, and so much progress has been made. That is true, but even with all this progress it's not easy to forget these experiences because they've shaped our lives and our identities. You can rationalize that the perpetrators were twisted and wicked, but this behavior did not stop when the civil rights bills were signed into law in the mid 1960s.

Chapter 7
LEARNING MY PLACE

THE GREATEST INFLUENCE of my years growing up was my mother and her faith. Mom was a committed Christian. She taught me about the Bible, and we would read it together. She was also a woman of prayer.

As I mentioned, I suffered from both asthma and epilepsy as a child, but she prayed and took God at His Word, refusing to receive anything less than my healing. In faith, my parents took me to an Oral Roberts crusade at the Milwaukee Arena when I was eight years old. There, after prayer and the laying-on of hands, God healed me of asthma. He was also faithful to heal me of my epilepsy, though it took a few years for the seizures to stop completely. By the time I was thirteen I was a healthy young man ready to face a whole new set of challenges: my teenage years.

Our family attended a church that was a merger between two congregations: a black Methodist and a Swedish Methodist church. However, my mother eventually became concerned that the gospel was not being preached there. She belonged to a Bible study group with women from different racial and ethnic backgrounds, and one of those friends attended a non-denominational evangelical church. Mom thought it would be good for me to get solid Bible instruction, so she began to take me to Racine Bible Church, dropping me off for Sunday school. Sometimes I would stay for the service as well. What a different experience it was from my parents' church. It was a much larger congregation with a large number of families with children my own age. My Sunday school teachers were some of the nicest people that I would ever meet, and the people were friendly and invited me to participate in activities outside of the church. Soon I started attending Youth for Christ, a program designed to give teens the chance to fellowship together through fun activities. I went tobogganing for the first time and got to try other things I never would have had the opportunity to do, such as skiing.

I was in ninth grade when a group from Youth for Christ was planning a ski trip to Rib Mountain in Wausau, Wisconsin. My parents were beginning to prosper a bit, so they could afford to pay for me to go. I was so excited! Not many kids from my neighborhood had an opportunity to do anything like this. It was a long trip from Racine to Wausau, and we would have to stay overnight in a hotel. I had never stayed in a hotel before. Most of my trips of any distance had been to visit relatives in the South.

As we arrived and got ready to bunk down for the night my friends were talking about how exciting skiing would be. The next morning we got up, had breakfast, and headed off to the mountain to go skiing, but sadly, I have to admit that I did not like skiing very much. I was not a fan of winter in the first place; I only tolerated snow, and I wasn't particularly athletic, so the constant falling into the frigid snow and getting back up did not appeal to me. In my frustration I decided to do something else. I went for a walk. Boy, was that a mistake!

Let me explain something about the state of Wisconsin in the 1960s. The demographic lines were very clearly defined. Black people mainly lived in Racine, Kenosha, Beloit, Milwaukee, and a few in Madison. At that time there were seventy-five thousand blacks in Wisconsin out of a total population of over four million people. A few black people lived in Green Bay, but most of them wore green-and-gold uniforms with numbers on the back when they went to work. (The Green Bay Packers!) A black person who left the cities in southern Wisconsin would leave all racial diversity behind. Even though I'd had prior experiences with racial prejudice it hadn't jaded me where white people were concerned. I was trusting enough to go skiing in an unfamiliar part of the state where I would be the only black person there.

I left the ski lodge and wandered down the road to clear my head. The road leading away from the lodge was a little narrow, but I was walking opposite the traffic. My boots didn't grip, so I was slipping as I walked, trying not to fall into the deep snow slightly off of the road. All at once I saw a car coming toward me. As it approached I could see that there were young people in it, and suddenly they swerved, veering toward me! As I jumped out of the way I fell face-first into the snow bank, and the people in the car rolled down the windows and yelled something at me. I stood up out of the dirty snow, angry and stunned. And I started to cry. Why would they try to run me down? What had I done to them? The answer to those questions was that I existed, and for some reason that was some kind of affront to them.

I rushed back to the ski lodge and remained there until the rest of the group was finished skiing. That evening I told the adult chaperones about my devastating experience. They were empathetic and tried to console me, but they couldn't realize how this experience reinforced a feeling that I would never fully be accepted, even among fellow Christians. I was the only black kid who attended this trip; in fact, I was the only black kid in the youth group. How could they have known what I was going through? I was dealing with the shock of it myself, not fully understanding why it was happening to me, and I simply couldn't explain it to anyone.

Another time when I was traveling on a bus to a recreational activity with the Youth for Christ group I struck up a conversation with a girl. After we talked awhile Wendy (not her real name) suddenly turned away from me and started looking out the window.

"I can't talk with you anymore," she said.

I was stumped. "Why not?" I asked.

"You might get the wrong idea," she said.

"What idea do you think I'm getting?" I wondered out loud.

"You act like you want to date me," she said.

Wendy was very attractive, but I didn't want to rush anything. After all, she might reject me. Before I could even respond she went on to explain, "I could never date you because it would be against the Bible."

I was flabbergasted. "Where in the Bible does it say that two human beings cannot date?" I asked.

She enlightened me. "According to the Bible, black people are cursed."

"What?" I exclaimed. "How is that?"

Wendy went on to tell me that Noah had a son, Ham, who saw his father drunk and naked, and when his father discovered this he cursed Ham's son Canaan and made him a slave to his brothers, Shem and Japheth. "Since black people descended from Ham and had been slaves in America, whites and blacks should never date or marry. As descendants of Ham, black people are cursed to always be slaves," she concluded.

I knew the Bible fairly well, but all of this stuff about Ham was new to me. When she talked about the curse of Ham I thought that she was talking about the fact that my people ate a high-fat diet with a lot of pork, thus the "curse of Ham."

"The Bible also says that you shouldn't be 'unequally yoked,'" she continued." I had a pretty good knowledge of the Bible, thanks to my mother, and was also pretty sure that black people were not cursed. I also remembered that the Bible had said not to be unequally yoked with unbelievers (2 Cor. 6:14). But I was a believer.

On top of this I had a more personal connection with interracial marriage. After completing his tour of duty in the air force my older brother Jim worked as an aide at a residential treatment center. It was there that he met a white woman from northern Wisconsin who would change his life. Patricia Stauber was a nurse, and although it was a tough time to be a pioneer in race relations they fell in love and got married in 1967. They endured all the stares and intrusive questions like, "What's going to happen to your children?" The answer then is what it still is today: "They will grow up!" The other commonly posed question was, "Who are your children going to marry?" The answer to that question is, "Other human beings!"

I would eventually find out that some of the kids that I went to Youth for Christ with attended a church that was doctrinally affiliated with Bob Jones University. Although the university has since retracted this policy, at the time they believed these spurious interpretations of Scripture and forbade the dating of people across racial lines. Wendy was not a Bible scholar, and she was just repeating what she'd been taught. I've seen her in the years since, and I know that she would be embarrassed if I reminded her about that conversation. As with many of the memories I'm recounting, I realize that many of the slights and rejections were not intentional. In fact, I believe most of the people involved in these circumstances would be amazed at the lasting impact that remains from these past interactions.

I don't mention these things to stir up hatred or animosity of any kind toward anybody. As a Christian I have consciously forgiven anyone who has wrongfully treated me, but as I recall these memories some of them have brought up dormant emotions that I thought were long gone. Now I am simply sharing them to illustrate that asking black people to forget about race and switch over to a focus on poverty as the primary cause of injustice just might not be an easy thing to do.

Would you ask a Jewish man to forget the Holocaust? Would you rebuke him, stating that it occurred a generation ago, that we have now progressed, and that the hatred and discrimination that spawned it is past? No, you wouldn't. Anti-Jewish sentiments are not dead, even in "enlightened" Western countries. Although the Holocaust ended by 1945, anti-Semitism clearly lives on.

The injustices black people faced in America began in 1620 with the advent of slavery, but the Thirteenth Amendment abolishing slavery wasn't adopted until over two hundred years later in 1865. Then it was another century before the Voting Rights Act of 1965 and other anti-discriminatory legislation were realized. Meanwhile, discriminatory practices have endured throughout this timeline despite the legal advances, and they continue in various forms to this day both on a societal level and in very personal ways. In the past, blacks grew up "knowing their place." For me, it was a learning curve.

Although I experienced some of my greatest joys during my junior high school years I wish I could tell you that most of them avoided the taint of race, but few of them did. These experiences, however—good and bad—helped to prepare me for leadership roles throughout my life. Little did I know at the time that it was God's plan to use me in various roles of racial reconciliation throughout my career.

While I was watching the events of the civil rights movement unfold in America, I was also studying racism at school. As I read *Cry, The Beloved Country* by Alan Paton I learned about apartheid in South Africa and found I could relate many of the events to America in the 1960s. I also became fascinated with Australia. How could a country that has something named a great white shark not fascinate you? But it was their immigration policy that really interested me. Australia, in the 1960s, was a country that was resource-rich but lacked the population to fully take advantage of the potential wealth that they could create. They desperately needed and wanted immigrants.

I thought it might be great to live in Australia, a place with koala bears, kangaroos, and crocodiles. As a teenager, I didn't think much about the logistics of such a plan, and I might have been all in except that their immigration policy forbade blacks from moving there. This overt discrimination made Australia seem like a twin to South Africa. They were both examples of governments that systematically created policies to restrict the lives of their citizens. This bothered me so much that when I got involved in the Model UN program in my high school I delighted in standing up and giving speeches that denounced any of the resolutions that came from diplomatic representatives of these two countries, even though we were only role-playing the drama as students. The Model UN allowed me, as a teenager, to exercise my displeasure with their brand of racism. But the lessons about race weren't confined to books or mock government. I encountered them in the school musical as well.

Christine Bissell believed in me. She was my music teacher in junior high. She was one of a kind and a little quirky, but she loved her students, and we knew it. She got me involved in music, which has proved to be a lifelong pleasure, thanks to her. She encouraged me to try out for the school musical in ninth grade, dedicating extra time to practice with me, and she kept trying to find the best piece of music for my audition. When the audition came I was very nervous, as it was the first time I would sing a solo before a group of peers. As I remember, I sang better than I had ever sung in my lifetime, and my classmates clapped for me. This audition and my previous lead role in the seventh-grade play *Peck's Bad Boy* helped me get the lead role as Uncle Chester in the musical *Get Up and Go!* My parents were very proud of me.

I was a shy kid and a bookworm to that point. The black kids in my neighborhood derisively called me "the Professor," but singing and acting in a musical was like living in another world. It helped to break me out of my shell and be someone different.

The year was 1967, and my old nemesis, race, came into play. Some of my classmates interjected race into this potentially wonderful experience and questioned how I, a black kid, was going to play the role of the uncle of another character who was white. The student who played my niece was named Margaret, and as I remember she was from one of the British Commonwealth countries, and she was beautiful. In the play there was no kissing, but I would have to hug her. Even though she was playing my niece, this was risqué for this time period.

Along with hugging Margaret I had to dance around and have a close friendship with another female classmate who played a custodian in the play. Although I might have expected some usual, garden-variety teasing that kids engage in at that age, what I encountered was some sarcasm and joking about the racial difference between my young female co-stars and myself. I came out of that experience with a love of music, a lack of fear when presenting before a crowd, and a sharper awareness of the distinctions that race can make between people. Years later the reality of those memories and the foolish distinctions of the times still bother me.

Chapter 8
THE PROFESSOR

WHEN I WAS a youngster I was a legitimate nerd apparently deserving of my nickname, the Professor. I loved science and wanted telescopes, microscopes, and chemistry sets for my birthdays. I read all the time, and from the time I was twelve years old I knew I wanted to go to college. Like other blacks who worked hard in school, I suffered through the accusations of "speaking white" and not being "black enough." In junior high school kids picked on me. As hard as it was to relate to white people at times, I experienced rejection from black kids as well. I remember one boy who sat behind me in class who would flick my ear while the teacher wasn't looking. I couldn't understand why he was treating me that way, especially since he was black. This went on for months, and I prayed daily that he would move. One day God had pity on me, and my tormenter moved away.

I wasn't the only one who was bullied though. I had a childhood friend who lived around the block. Gracie was a bright student and very beautiful, but like me, she found it hard to fit in. She was black, but she came to class with blonde hair once. Another time she came to school in an outfit that was fringed, dressing up like a Native American. Some kids made fun of her for her unusual flair, but I kind of understood her. She was trying to find her identity, and so was I. I wanted to know who I was, and I hated being ridiculed and minimized.

It's significant to note that during those years America

was hotly debating whether or not blacks should assimilate into the white culture. While many blacks sought integration, there was also a black Muslim movement promoting independence from whites educationally and economically. For the longest time it was really a moot point, as many whites did not want blacks to assimilate into their culture; they were comfortable if blacks just stayed to themselves socially and economically. This is the choice that my parents and their generation faced.

I was raised in a family that wanted to become middle class. My parents understood that in order to succeed in America you had to learn the ways of the dominant culture, even if that culture was not accepting of you. Proper English, proper manners, and proper dress were required because they would open the door to opportunity as wide as it was going to open.

Because I was an individual who adopted both black and white culture I never really fit in with either group, and this was particularly painful growing up. One of my most vivid memories from high school was of the cool black guys standing at the bottom of the stairs by the library leaning up against a heating vent.

"Professor!" I heard them call to me, taunting. "What are you doing after you graduate?"

"Man," I said, "I'm going to college. I just don't know where."

One of the cool guys looked at me and sneered. "You ain't going nowhere!" he said. "You're just gonna live in the hood. You ain't nothing!"

I told them that I was going to succeed and be somebody. This exchange stuck with me because it was different from what I knew of other ethnic groups. It seemed that others understood this principle: *a rising tide lifts all boats.* They understood that the success of a few helped make the success of many possible. I saw this demonstrated by the people in my own neighborhood. I knew Jewish people who worked hard to promote opportunities for other Jews, immigrants from Yugoslavia who brought over other members of their families, friends who would bring friends over from "the old countries" and help them get settled in America. I won't win a popularity contest by saying this, but in the black community I saw an attempt by my people to keep each other down, especially among those of my generation. It's like what happens with a pot of crayfish. It seems that when one is about to climb out of the pot another reaches up, grabs hold of him with his pincher, and then pulls him back into the pot with the rest.

Years later I ran into one of my tormentors from the neighborhood. I was a principal at the time, taking kids from my school on a field trip to the Milwaukee Museum. We were in the dinosaur section when I looked up and saw him, and he came over to say hello and introduced me to his fiancée.

"A lot of things are going good for me," he said. "I'm going to college now and trying to make something of myself," he told me.

"That's really good. I'm happy for you," I replied.

"Listen, man," he said. "I want to say I'm sorry for the way I treated you when we were growing up. It was stupid."

His apology caught me by surprise, and although it was sincere my inner reaction was not charitable. I thought to myself, "If you had used your energy studying instead of making fun of me you would have finished your college degree years ago and would have enjoyed some success earlier." Instead I just told him that I hoped he would succeed and that I was glad to hear he was going to school.

My parents had taught me that when another crayfish is trying to climb out of the pot, let him climb out. Don't pull him back in.

While some blacks saw assimilation as a way to move ahead, others—wanting to maintain their black identity—found themselves stranded, stuck on the rung of the ladder that they were born on. It separated some blacks into different classes. It was similar to the lives of field slaves and house slaves of an age past. If you were a house slave your station on your master's property would have seemed to put you in a higher position than the poor field slave. You would have dressed much better and eaten much better than the slave in the field. As a house slave you might have chosen to be compliant and obedient, thinking that at least it would lead to better treatment than field slaves received. In time you might feel superior to the field slave, mistaking these refinements as a statement of your worth, but you would still be a slave. In the same way, a field slave, seeing the much easier life of the house slave, could become resentful. Feeling hopeless, he might have tried to escape, taking any opportunity to run away. The house slave was just as trapped in hopelessness. Neither of them enjoyed true freedom. A prisoner in nice prison clothes is still in prison. Resenting another prisoner because they have nicer clothes is an exercise in futility. Though I have used this metaphor from slavery, many blacks today resent those who have become successful and see them as nothing but house slaves.

Chapter 9
GUESS WHO'S COMING
FOR CHRISTMAS?

I T WAS THE 1970s, and attitudes about dating and marriage were—shall we say—*carefree*. I was in my junior
and senior years of undergraduate school at the University of Wisconsin–Eau Claire, and I was dating a young
lady. We wanted to be married, and being raised old fash-
ioned I knew I would have to ask her father's permission.
I believed that you don't just marry a person; you also
marry their family.

I figured marriage would be tough, especially if it was
an interracial marriage, but I did not believe race should
determine who you loved, dated, or married. You see,
at this point I really wanted to practice what I believed.
Dating a black, white, Hispanic, or Asian woman was all
the same to me if we had similar interests and liked each
other. Unfortunately, I was of the minority opinion.

I remember that night. She lived about an hour north of
the university in a very small town. It was Christmas vacation, and I was really nervous. This was a big, life-defining
moment! It was an extremely cold winter night, with tem-
peratures below zero, but I didn't realize the reception I
was about to receive was going to be more frigid than the
temperature.

Looking back, it reminds me of the 1968 movie *Guess
Who's Coming to Dinner*. The controversial film is a story
of an accomplished black man (played by Sidney Poitier)
and a wealthy young white woman (Katherine Houghton)

seeking the blessing of their parents in their desire to marry. As in the movie, my girlfriend's white parents were not prepared to meet a black fiancé. I think I would have been a good catch in most cases—a good student with a bright future ahead of me—but that was not good enough.

When we arrived her parents were polite but guarded. I think they had guessed what we were there for. I asked to speak with her father alone, and he led me out to his office, which was located in their barn. I remember shaking as I was talking. I was scared.

After addressing him politely I told him, "Your daughter and I have been dating for the last two years. I love her, and I want to marry her." I could tell by his face that he was not thrilled. He didn't get angry or overly demonstrative, but he said in a very matter-of-fact manner, "I wish that you wouldn't." He explained that it wasn't personal but that it was more about the situation and the hardships that we would face. He was straightforward about his opposition. Discouraged and defeated, I walked into the house and looked at my girlfriend. It was a great disappointment. I had experienced rejection before that time and have experienced it since, but that kind of rebuff was a hard pill to swallow. To be told that I wasn't good enough to marry someone because of my race wounded me deeply.

After that we went through a period where we broke up and then reconciled, and I asked her to marry me despite her parents' objection. We were serious enough that we moved her possessions to the city where I lived. She, however, remained in another city where she worked. I was working with high school kids in a Fellowship of Christian Athletes group, but somehow going to church and being around kids who were not that much younger than myself compounded my loneliness. Even worse, the rejection from her parents festered in me, and I felt that their disapproval of me was impossible to get around; the damage had been done. What I didn't realize was that God was working behind the scenes.

It was during this time that I met Peggy. Peggy had been raised in a Christian home and had committed her life to Christ as a young child. As with many of us who were raised under similar circumstances, she grew up, finished college, and drifted away from her relationship with Jesus. She married her high school sweetheart, expecting to be married for the rest of her life, but after a few years her husband fell in love with a coworker and divorced her.

Peggy had been taught that divorce was shameful and an unpardonable sin. She believed that she had failed God by being divorced. She felt like a second-class citizen. Satan—the enemy of our souls—capitalized on her misconception and condemnation to make her feel that God would never accept her. Without hope a person makes horrible, destructive choices, and Peggy began to party and live a lifestyle that was foreign to her upbringing.

She was a teacher professionally, but she had wandered spiritually. She looked at other religions hoping to find peace, but her search just accentuated her loneliness and emptiness. One of her friends, sensing that she really wasn't into the party lifestyle, told her that she needed to "get in" or "get out." She decided to get out.

A few weeks later she was fixing breakfast on a Sunday morning for her sister and brother-in-law, who were visiting her that weekend. Suddenly, she heard a quiet voice inside of her. "Go to your parents' church," it told her.

She argued back.

"I'm estranged from my parents and don't want to go to their church."

The voice kept on, insisting that she go. She silently argued with it for about an hour, but she finally gave in and went to the church. Although the service was almost over when she arrived, her dad, who happened to be ushering that Sunday, was shocked to see her. As she stood there, the same inner *voice* directed her view to the front of the church. "You have to speak to one of those three men in the front," it said.

As the service ended and the sanctuary began to clear, *the voice* said, "You need to talk to that one," indicating which of the three she was to speak to. She milled around for a minute or two but figured since she had come this far she might as well follow through. She went up to the man and said, "Hello, my name is Margaret Might."

I was that man. "This is a little strange," I thought to myself. She seemed shy and a little embarrassed when she did this, and we only talked for a minute or two. We would later discover that our parents were friends at church.

Later that day she called me. She talked about her need to reconnect with the Lord Jesus. We went out to dinner that evening at Ponderosa Steakhouse, and we talked for hours about her spiritual condition. She was a mess! I drove her to her apartment, where our conversation continued, and I told her that she needed to give her life back to the Lord.

Peggy recommitted her life to Christ and started to read the Bible again. She soon became filled with the Holy Spirit and embraced the charismatic move of God, which was very important to me. What began to grow in my mind was the absolute commitment that Peggy had to the Lord. We started going to meetings together, but I had a problem: I was still engaged to another woman. As hurtful as it was, I knew that I couldn't marry my girlfriend. After we broke up, Peggy and I began to date, and we were married a few months later. We faced some opposition from some Christians we knew, but it was more about the fact that Peggy had been divorced than about the difference in our races. Despite that, we had the blessing of our parents, who supported us from day one. Forty years later we are still happily married.

Chapter 10
A SLICE OF HEAVEN

URING OUR EARLY years as we were building a life together we didn't have to face racial conflicts within our family, but that didn't mean it was easy. It was the 1970s, and the change in society was proceeding slowly. One painful memory was an experience we had in New Orleans where we chaperoned a church youth group with our friends. I had resolved several years before that I hated the South and would not go there under any circumstance, but since the Gustafsons were close friends and it was a Christian conference we decided to go.

After eating in a restaurant in the downtown area we went to the counter to pay. The lady behind the counter looked at me and then looked at Peggy with disgust. I gave the lady my money. She figured out the change and then threw the money at me. I stooped down to pick up some of the change. When I walked out it was like an epiphany. "The South is still a despicable place!" I told myself.

Shortly after we married we lived in Sterling, Kansas, a small town of about eighteen hundred people where we both worked for a Presbyterian college. We knew that it was God's will for us to move there. Generally, we did not feel completely self-conscious about having a mixed marriage, but occasionally it would surface at places like basketball or football games. Walking through large crowds was like walking the gauntlet. It was the support of our pastors in our church that allowed us to find an oasis of love and acceptance.

Prior to our move Peggy and I attended a national charismatic conference in Kansas City, Missouri. That was one of the best weeks of our lives. We camped about fifty miles away from Kansas City, and there were lots of "crazy charismatics" camping at the same campsite. We met Spirit-filled believers from different races and denominations from all over the country. Lifting our hands and singing, we worshiped together at the campsite after the evening meetings at Arrowhead Stadium, basking in the presence of God.

In Kansas we started looking for a church. After attending the charismatic conference and worshiping with believers from every tribe and tongue and people and nation, earthly divisions and distinctions were trivial to us. We longed for a church that really reflected the kingdom of God, where Jesus was preached and His presence was almost tangible. We wanted lively and vibrant worship, and we wanted to see the gifts of the Spirit evident all of the time, not just when a special ministry came through. We wanted what we saw at the conference in Kansas City! We looked for months, meanwhile hosting a Bible study in our home near the college. A young pastor from Hays, Kansas, traveled sixty miles from his home to meet with us weekly. He told us about a church that was pastored by his mentor, Fred Kirkpatrick.

The next Sunday we couldn't wait to get to Faith Community Church in Great Bend, Kansas. We arrived a little early. It was a quaint little white church that seated about two hundred people, but the only seats available were along the back wall near the door. Sunday school was still going on. The pastor came out and insisted that all of the adults join the children in singing the song "Father Abraham." This may seem strange, but it spoke to us. "There is no pretension here," we thought. The people swung their right arms, left arms, and all of the other motions associated with that simple chorus. When the regular service started the praise was wonderful. There wasn't the usual diminishing participation you see in churches, with a few lively rows of worshippers up front petering out as you look toward the back of the church. No spectators here! Even in the back people were clapping, shouting, raising their hands, and praising God. After this there was a message in tongues. Some sick people were prayed for with the laying on of hands, and there were prophetic words. Following this, Pastor Fred began to preach. His message was simple yet very powerful. I heard a message that was completely centered on Jesus and grounded in the Bible.

After the service the pastor stood at the back door to shake hands. When Peggy and I approached he turned to me and said, "Sometime you will have to preach here." This was so strange. He had never met us! How could he know that God had been speaking to us about future ministry and our calling? Even so, I really had nothing to preach. In one service I had seen demonstrated most of the things that I knew. What could I possibly contribute? I smiled weakly and told him that we would be back the next Sunday, and I kept my word.

After a few months we were going to most of the weekly meetings that Pastor Fred and his wife, Sally, held. We even traveled with them to some regional meetings in places like Pratt and Bunker Hill. We met some very dear believers, like Alan and Lynn Webb, who became very special to us. Spiritually hungry, we wanted Jesus and the Word of God. In all of these meetings, even though it was a white congregation, we met brothers and sisters who knew us only as Milt and Peggy—not *black Milt* and his wife, *white Peggy*. We saw such affection toward us that it gave me insight into what the kingdom of God could really be like here on Earth.

Getting to know Fred and Sally became be a pivotal point in our lives. Outside of our parents, no one else had as much godly influence on us, including the example of a strong marriage, to give us a good start as newlyweds. By the way, I did preach in their church and some others in Hays, Ness City, and Leoti in Kansas. The confidence that they showed in us has carried us through till today. With the support of Fred and Sally, Peggy and I returned to Racine and started a charismatic church. The first members of the church were a group of young people we had discipled before we left for Kansas. They were growing up and excited that we were coming home to start a work.

Over time we began to attract a multi-racial congregation. Mixed couples, Hispanic members, and others found a home there. Race did not play a negative role in the relationships of the church. We worshiped God together and loved one another. One member said that if she wanted to think about me as a black man she would have to consciously think about it. This was not a denial of reality; it was an affirmation of what the Bible teaches and a living-out of the gospel. In the kingdom of God there are no Jews or Greeks, males or females, black or white. (See Galatians 3:28.)

Throughout the twenty years of the church we developed close relationships, saw lives change, and made plenty of mistakes. I returned to my career path as an educator, but I never lost the desire to pastor a New Testament church that displays the God who loves people from every nation and kindred.

Chapter 11
"THE COUSINS"

BECAUSE I HAD friends from across the color spectrum growing up I had to abide being called an Uncle Tom by some other blacks. I didn't care what color my friends were if I deemed them worth hanging out with. I still feel that way. The term *Uncle Tom* was meant to frighten me back to the herd—to make me seek refuge and stay close to my own kind—but it didn't endear me to the guys from my neighborhood. It was like being called a house slave, and it is extremely offensive to any black person.

In the days when I grew up the label was used to demean educated blacks who wanted to escape the poverty they inherited and to be somebody, but that use of the term is a sign of ignorance. The novel *Uncle Tom's Cabin* by Harriet Beecher Stowe was the second-best seller of the nineteenth century, only exceeded by the Bible in sales. The mistreatment of Uncle Tom and the portrayal of his sufferings at the hand of the overseer, Simon Legree, were so graphic that they clearly displayed the plight of the black slave to a white audience. His longsuffering in the face of such unjust treatment awakened an outrage in those who wouldn't have otherwise given the plight of the black man a second thought.

For many who were not abolitionists, *Uncle Tom's Cabin* stirred their consciences and made them realize that the institution of slavery was a plague upon America that needed to be eliminated. This work of literature raised the issue to such a degree that it is considered to be one of the last straws that broke the back of slavery in America. In fact, along with other contributors, this book was believed to be one of the sparks that led to the Civil War. Without this wonderful work by Ms. Stowe, the emancipation of all black slaves might have been delayed further.

Despite improvements in race relations, Americans have not outgrown name-calling, even between blacks. Supreme Court Justice Clarence Thomas has been referred to as an Uncle Tom by some blacks who have a national audience. It must seem really strange to people of other ethnicities that blacks would cannibalize one of their own who has reached such a lofty position. Instead they watch as some prominent blacks reach up and try to grab Justice Thomas and pull him back into the pot with the other crayfish.

Jesus said, "If a house is divided against itself, that house cannot stand" (Mark 3:25, NIV). This scripture refers to the power of people in agreement. In the Genesis 11 story of the Tower of Babel, God commented that if they are in agreement, men can accomplish anything. (See verse 6.) In the New Testament Jesus affirmed this kingdom principle when He said, "Again, truly I tell you that if two of you on earth agree about anything they ask for, it will be done for them by my Father in heaven" (Matthew 18:19, NIV). But it's impossible to take advantage of the power of agree-ment when you default to backbiting and name-calling. Unfortunately this behavior has relegated my people to the role of the underclass, as they watch those who come to this country in poverty climb the ladder of success, step-ping over the rung that many blacks are stuck on.

The complexity of black-on-black relationships is a con-cept my brother Junior refers to as dealing with *the cousins*.

He used this term with me when I took a job as a super-intendent in a school district in Illinois. It was a challenge, as the graduation rate was very low and very few kids went to college, but I thought the job would be a good fit for me. The school board was made up of six black members and one white. I thought being a black superintendent coming from a district where we worked hard to raise the achievement of black students would make this a good situation to be in. I also felt that I could be a good role model for the kids. I was wrong.

From the moment I arrived it was déjà vu with a few new wrinkles. I heard racist comments from various people about my white wife. I had to hire most of the administrative team, and I hired a high school principal from an adjoining district who was recommended by the outstanding black superintendent of that district. The new principal happened to be white, and a rumor spread throughout the district that he was my nephew and that is why I hired him. At first I was confused about the rumor. I thought, "How could I have a white nephew?" Then it dawned on me: Peggy's side of the family! I guess I forgot that my wife was white! I was shocked that these people would be so hung up on the race of a few people when their situation was so dire. We had much bigger fish to fry.

All of this seemed so ignorant to me that it created a hostile, intolerable environment. Board members argued openly during school board meetings, some almost coming to blows. This district had a reputation of dysfunction and even corruption. Representatives from the state who had taken over the management of this district witnessed this behavior for at least a year before my arrival, and nothing was done. I wondered if they would have allowed this kind of dysfunction to reach that level if the district had been composed of primarily white students.

In the end the state identified me as the problem and got rid of me. I had only been there a year, but it shouldn't have surprised me since I was the twenty-first superintendent in nineteen years. Though I begged the state to make changes to the school board prior to this, the appeal fell on deaf ears. This incident occurred in one of the most liberal states in the Union. The practices I witnessed were counterproductive to the success of black people, as evidenced in Illinois' high black unemployment rate, deplorable black homicide rate, and low-ranking graduation rate.

Junior would simply say, "It's the cousins!" and I began to understand what he meant. Some people mistakenly perceive that black people think as a group, but blacks are not some kind of monolithic people with a *groupthink* phenomenon. The differences between the experiences and perspectives of blacks should not be a surprise since we are as diverse in all areas as whites. I can, however, understand why people misperceive this. The most prominent blacks that the media portrays seem to represent only a liberal viewpoint. Polls on the number of blacks who vote Democratic infer that all of us do, but as you will see from my own brothers in a later chapter, we split down the middle regarding our political affiliations.

Some black Christians who hold strong convictions about abortion, gay marriage, and other moral issues compromise those biblical convictions to vote for candidates whose views are hostile to those same biblical truths. I have watched this for a number of years, and I know that the Democratic Party counts on that kind of duplicity in every election. They assume that blacks will follow them, period. It doesn't matter if they are Christians or not. I have watched these same churches and pastors rationalize how they, like Esau, have sold their birthright for a few meager creature comforts that politicians promise them. Most of those comforts have not materialized, so they have made this Faustian bargain for nothing.

I look forward to the day when my people break free from *the cousins* and vote according to their values, especially those who profess to be Christians. I have waited a long time for this and have been extremely disappointed. I have wanted them to at least make politicians earn their vote and not take them for granted.

About ten years ago, before President Obama was in office, my congressman, Paul Ryan, invited me to attend a conference in Washington, DC. Former Senator Kay Bailey Hutchison of Texas and Senator Rick Santorum of Pennsylvania hosted it. All of the roughly five hundred attendees were black and Republican, and they were some of the smartest people I have ever met. We listened to speeches by people like Michael Steele, who was then the lieutenant governor of Maryland, and Franklin Raines, who was the head of Fannie Mae at the time.

One of the attendees, the head of the state black caucus in Florida, told me about a large meeting she'd had with both Republican and Democrat Hispanic leaders in her state. When they discussed various issues of interest to Hispanics they were not committed to one political party over the other. The Hispanic attendees explained that they were focused on the issues so as not to be taken for granted by either political party. Knowing that the majority of blacks were voting for Democrats, they perceived that blacks were being taken for granted and their issues were not being taken seriously anymore. As a result, the Hispanic group was courted and taken seriously by both parties. Sound bites and cries of racism didn't cause these intelligent people to budge from taking an independent stance. She told me that she wished that black people would take a similar position.

While visiting the offices of members of Congress during this trip to DC, our group of black Republicans noticed few people of color on any senator's staff—both Republicans and Democrats. Our group sent word to the sponsors of our conference that this was unacceptable, reprimanding them for not making their rhetoric and overtures toward black people match their practices. The exception to this state of affairs was noticeably Kay Bailey Hutchison's staff, which contained blacks and Hispanics, and not just by a token number. She stood out among her colleagues and earned my immediate respect. Leaving that conference propelled me down the road of becoming less and less political. The hypocrisy of both parties was in danger of making me cynical about the country rather than the political system. I had to separate politics from my search for a real personal identity.

Chapter 12
IRISH FOR GOOD MEASURE

Assimilation has a long history in America. Every group that immigrated to the United States had a difficult choice to make. The dilemma has been, "How do I hold on to my cultural distinctiveness and yet move up the ladder?" Whenever a previously despised group moved up the ladder they became a part of the dominant culture and required some homage from the newest despised group. If they received that homage they might hold the ladder, at least a little bit, for that new group so that they could start that climb. Assimilation was the homage that was required. The Irish had to. The Polish and Italians did too. The interesting thing was that if you were darker you could not assimilate as easily. The darker your skin was—no matter your ethnicity—the longer your acceptance took.

People of black heritage who are extremely light skinned can pass in many situations. This has been true for a long time in America. Dark-skinned blacks who attempted to escape during slavery stood out wherever they went, but if their skin was light enough they may have been able to hide out in plain sight or even escape. What complicates the matter is that given the history of America there are very few black people who are exclusively African in their ancestry, and there are others who hail from other parts of the world, such as the West Indies. Thomas Jefferson's illegitimate children with black slaves could pass for white. Eston Hemings, one of the descendants of Jefferson's mistress, Sally Hemings, was half white. He lived in Madison, Wisconsin, in 1852, and no one knew that he had black heritage. At that time this was a tremendous advantage for him.

In 2010 PBS aired a documentary called *Faces of America* in which an African-American Harvard professor Henry Louis Gates Jr. used genetic markers to trace his ancestry. His search led him to distant relatives in a tribe in Africa, as well as a pub in Ireland. It was fascinating to watch but not surprising. At some point in the past a slave owner who was Irish had his way with Gates's great-great-great-great-grandmother. Daily I see the same type of dual identity. I look down at the back of my hands, and I see freckles. Even the name Thompson is a remnant from one of my ancestors, who took on the surname of his master.

Race is a very complex issue, and one of its strange dynamics is how perceptions about race are associated with the skin tones of people not only across racial lines but also within the same people group. A famous study known as the Clark Doll Experiment illustrates this point, and its results affected the outcome of the landmark 1954 civil rights case *Brown v. the Board of Education*, which challenged racial segregation in public schools. In 1939 Dr. Kenneth Clark, a black psychologist, did an experiment in which he presented black children with the choice of two dolls, one black and the other white. When the child was asked which doll was pretty, most said the white doll. They were then asked which doll was ugly, and most chose the black doll. Next they were asked, "Which doll is good?" Again, the white doll prevailed, while the black doll was seen as bad.

In the *Brown v. Board* case the results of this experiment were presented to the court by Thurgood Marshall, the plaintiff's lawyer and future Supreme Court justice. He wanted to demonstrate the destructive effect of separate-but-equal discrimination on the self-image of black children. In writing the legal opinion of the court's decision, Chief Justice Earl Warren specifically pointed to the Clark Doll Experiment as proof of the psychological damage done to black children by segregation. The Supreme Court unanimously ruled in favor of Brown, deeming state-sanctioned school segregation unconstitutional.

Interestingly, when an update to this study was sponsored by CNN in 2010, similar results were found.[1] Child development specialist Dr. Margaret Beale Spencer showed cartoon pictures to one hundred and thirty-three children from ages four through ten. The cartoons portrayed children of six different skin tones, from white to very dark. Interestingly, 82 percent of the white participants and 86 percent of the black participants showed a bias toward lighter skin tones being identified with good. Further, 66 percent of white children and 61 percent of black children chose the two darkest skin tones as undesirable. But even more telling, 82 percent of black participants and 100 percent of white participants identified pictures of children with middle and lighter skin tones as smart.

For many of us, our attitudes about race were formed when we were young, especially by middle school. How do children who carry these perceptions into adulthood knowingly or unknowingly perpetuate discrimination on a subconscious level? Think, for a moment, if you were a black participant with a dark complexion in this study. Your choices demonstrate two things: first, that if you could you would be a different color than you are, and second, and more destructively, you perceive that you are overwhelmingly considered unattractive and unintelligent by virtue of your God-given skin tone. Since this is a recent study it unfortunately affirms that negative perceptions about race and color are still with us more than six decades after Dr. Clark's initial study.

These studies are more than dry facts and statistics. They are the backstories of people of color all across our nation, and to understand how much perceptions about skin tone affect the lives of real children I only have to look at my own four sons and their perceptions of themselves.

Our oldest son, Nathanael, is black. We adopted him when he was twenty-one days old, and his biological mother and father are African Americans. Nathanael is darker than any of our other sons, who are mixed. Nate, as he is called, doesn't see people through the filter of race; his friends span the spectrum of races. This has been true since he was a child, as his experiences have shaped his perception of people.

His adoptive mother, Peggy, is white. His grandparents and aunts and uncles on his mother's side were white. He went to a Christian school, and many of his friends were white. But as he became a teenager his behavior changed. He decided to join a gang, and to prove that race didn't matter to him he joined the Latin Kings. Now that he's an adult we kid about it. I told him that at least he joined a gang that was equal opportunity!

Though Nate has been open in his acceptance of people, it has not always been reciprocated by society at large. Police have regularly stopped him. He looks like any other young black man in his early thirties, like a member of the hip-hop generation. Until he got a full-time job eight years ago he would wear his pants low (a fashion statement that I still fail to understand). He also had gold caps put on his teeth. Once when a police officer stopped him for speeding Nate responded politely to him, stating that he was sorry but needed to get to work. The officer said, "You have a job! Where?" This kind of situation has happened multiple times, including in our own neighborhood, when a police officer asked him what he was doing there. He explained that he was visiting his parents, but the officer did not believe him.

When Nate was hired by the school district as a custodian in 2008 he said people expected him to be ignorant or stupid. His appearance caused people to discount and stereotype him, but once they found out that he was articulate and personable, things changed.

Our next son, Matthew, is lighter than Nate. Matt is more Middle Eastern in appearance, and his attitude toward race is a mixed bag. Matt hates feeling like a victim just because he is half black. He calls himself a liberal, but he is more conservative than I am when it comes to race. Matt holds some beliefs that I held when I was younger— idealistic and believing that everything should be a meritocracy. I hated to check a race box on a form, especially if it was going to give me an undeserved break. Matt is like that. He doesn't want to use his race to open the door to opportunity. He is almost a straight-A student in undergraduate school, but he does not want to pursue financial aid if it comes to him on the basis of his race. In Matt's thinking, it would make the playing field uneven, and he would be taking something from another deserving student. The thing that Matt and I have discussed over and over is whether or not the playing field *is* even.

I have explained to him that, until recently, blacks were not afforded the same opportunities as whites. I am not trying to make him a victim of racism, but I am trying to help him feel less guilty about any opportunities that come to him to balance the lack of opportunities that he is heir to simply because of his race. If this raises the question of minority entitlement I would like to assert that there's an issue of entitlement that's accrued to white people simply because of their race. At the very least they escaped legal and custom-based discrimination that would have limited their opportunities, as it did with blacks. Further, racial discrimination is a reality with generational consequences both economically and socially.

Our son Thomas is probably the lightest of the boys. In fact, he could pass for white or some other ethnic group. Tom's first encounter with race is really telling. When he was in primary school his teacher reported some strange behavior to us. Tom refused to stand next to or drink water from the same fountain as a classmate of his, Delilah. Delilah was black. The teacher was perplexed because Tom had a black father and a white mother.

When Tom got home that day we asked him why he didn't like Delilah. He said that it was because she was black. We explained to Tom that he was black. That did not register with him. Tom said that he came from mom and that Nate and Matt, who were darker, came from me. We were shocked and a little amused at his reasoning. It took a while before Tom came to realize that he was half black.

Through the years Tom has had friends of different races but spends more time with whites. He has a bachelor's degree from the University of Wisconsin–Madison and a master's degree from New York University. He lives in Manhattan but works in the Bronx as a teacher. He lives his sense of social responsibility by helping disabled children of various races who live in poverty. Tom and I had not talked in depth about how he perceives race as an adult until recently. He shared with me how he felt as a mixed kid in Advanced Placement courses without any black classmates in a diverse school. He also told me of his experiences in New York.

Tom has white friends in New York who've gone through periods of unemployment and were broke. When he asked them why they didn't just temporarily take a job in fast food they laughed and told him that their mothers would be ashamed of them. Though he eats in a variety of restaurants in New York, Tom says he's never seen a white person who was not in a managerial position in these fast food restaurants. The lower workers are people of color. I think my son can give me insight into what it's like to be biracial, though I am still trying to discover what it means to be black.

Our youngest son, Daniel, looks almost southern European, Amish, or White. He has a long beard, like a member of ZZ Top, and dresses sort of like a hipster with a Rat Pack type of hat. He is a newspaper editor in northwest Indiana. Daniel has friends from all different racial and ethnic groups, and I think he identifies more with being mixed. His one tether to his black identity was his relationship with my parents. He spent a lot of time with them when he was very young, staying overnight with them at their apartment. He grew up eating collard greens, black-eyed peas, and cornbread and hearing stories about their background. Daniel's understanding of black culture comes primarily from them.

He shared an experience that he had when he worked as an editor in far western Nebraska a few years ago. He was eating in a restaurant when another patron began staring at him. Daniel wanted to avoid eye contact because he figured this guy was going to approach him with personal questions, but he couldn't help himself. He looked up.

As if on cue, the guy immediately shouted across the restaurant, and without batting an eye he asked Daniel, "What are you?" Daniel was shocked and thought that it was direct and really strange. He wanted to give a sarcastic answer like, "I'm a human being." Instead, he indulged him by sharing our Heinz 57 ethnic background.

"It's very interesting," he told him. "I am part African American, Choctaw, German, and even a little Irish." The man looked at him with wonder and amazement. When he told me about it I thought it was funny since we have no Irish blood in us, but Daniel said he threw in Irish for good measure.

When I started to write this book both Thomas and Daniel wanted me to relate something they experienced in high school. Thomas graduated in 2003 from Washington Park High School in Racine, a diverse school with a significant population of black students. Because we relocated to Kenosha during his high school years, Daniel attended Tremper High, located in a less diverse school zone, graduating in 2007. Both sons took Advanced Placement courses in high school, top-level courses that can lead to college credit if passed successfully.

Neither of my sons had any other black students in these courses. They noticed that most of the black students were in the high school regular track, which was not college preparatory. This meant that a lot of those students were not going to go to college, or if they did they would have difficulty, not being adequately prepared.

My sons were not being arrogant or condescending; they were only making an observation. They said that they felt awkward being the only students of color, but they also knew that if they were going to go to college they would have to get over it. This choice sounded very similar to the one that I had made years before when there were very few black guys in my college prep classes, or even at college for that matter.

Even though Thomas and Daniel both attended the University of Wisconsin–Madison, they would bemoan the same experience there. Among tens of thousands of students very few were black—not much different than when I was in college decades earlier. It seems that where race and higher education are concerned in Wisconsin, the more things change, the more they stay the same. There were about one thousand African-American students out of a student body of approximately forty-two thousand students.[2] As recently as 2013, only 2 percent of undergraduate students at UW–Madison were black, and 3 percent were of two or more races, compared to 76 percent white.[3] Although the campus draws students from across the nation, blacks represented 6.3 percent of the general population in Wisconsin in 2010, and whites represented 86 percent.[4] Even in a more diverse community like Milwaukee there is a disparity. UW–Milwaukee had 8 percent black undergraduate students in a city that's over 39.97 percent black.[5]

Although some of my experiences are similar to those of my sons, they are indicative of the next generation when it comes to their own concepts of race. Their impressions about race are different from mine, with the exception of Nate. Maybe his experiences parallel mine because we are about the same skin tone. When he goes out people know that he is black. It is the same with me.

Chapter 13
MY BROTHERS AND THE SUCCESS OF MY FAMILY

U NLIKE MANY BLACK kids growing up today, I had both a mother and a father in the home. A lot of my friends were members of two-parent families as well. In 1960 about one out of four black kids was born out of wedlock.[1] We were fortunate compared to today, when almost 75 percent of black babies born in America are growing up in single-parent homes.[2]

The stories of my brothers and what they have accomplished validates the sacrifice our parents made to provide a better life for all of us. In essence our parents set the table for the next generation to succeed. In my family we came in pairs. My step-brothers, Lewis and Linton, were about twenty years older than me. My brothers James and Arzell were about ten years older. Then Stan and I came along. My older brothers' experiences vary from mine because all of them were born in the South and were impacted by growing up there.

LINTON

Linton was the second eldest son in our family. He was my step-brother and nineteen years older than me. Because he married and moved his family to California when I was around five years old I never really got to know him. I saw him only once or twice until he passed away unexpectedly when I was in my mid-twenties.

LEWIS

My oldest brother, Lewis, moved from the South after serving in the military during the time of the Korean War. He and Linton both served in the army during that time. When Lewis married, he and his wife, Heddy, moved north to Racine, where he worked at Belle City with our dad. As Dad was five years younger than my mother, Lewis and Dad had a unique relationship. In time they were like brothers, though Lewis treated him with the respect of a father.

Lewis and Heddy worked hard and prospered. Heddy worked in the personnel department for Southern Wisconsin Center, a treatment facility for the severely mentally disabled. Lewis also had an entrepreneurial streak. He grew vegetables and sold them at his own stand on the south side of the city. I knew a lot about Lewis and Heddy because a few years after my parents bought their first house on St. Patrick Street, Lewis and Heddy bought the house next door, so I grew up next door to my oldest brother. His oldest children were my closest playmates. Since these three children were girls and my family had only boys, my nieces were like the sisters I never had. We walked to school together, shared a swing set in their back-yard, and fought together. If we misbehaved Lewis would spank us. Since Lewis had nine children I was never alone or had a lack for kids to play with. Lewis' greatest influence on me was in the area of my faith.

When he was young Lewis was pretty wild. I have been told that he was a serious drinker. Then someone shared the gospel with him, and he has said that it changed his life. Lewis attended a meeting where the preacher shared a scripture that would shape his beliefs for the rest of his life. That scripture was in Mark 16:17–18: "And these signs will accompany those who believe: In my name they will drive out demons; they will speak in new tongues; they will pick up snakes with their hands; and when they drink deadly poison, it will not hurt them at all; they will place their hands on sick people, and they will get well" (NIV).

This resonated in his heart. Lewis became a Pentecostal Christian and attended the Church of God in Christ, a black Pentecostal denomination. It's important for the reader to understand the background of Pentecostal Christianity as it relates to race. When the Pentecostal movement started in the early 1900s at Azusa Street it was multi-racial. People from every race and ethnicity were being saved and baptized in the Holy Spirit. The leadership of the movement was both black and white. It seemed like heaven had come to Earth. Human divisions seemed to fall away. Then the devil intervened with a very easy attack. He used the racial separation and discrimination that was happening in society at large and brought it into the church. In time, the Pentecostal movement divided along racial lines into three denominations: the Assemblies of God, Apostolic Pentecostal Church, and the Church of God in Christ. The Church of God in Christ became the place most black Pentecostals attended since they were not fully welcome in the others at that time. Sadly, the church lost its ability to demonstrate that the love of God was beyond earthly divisions and distinctions such as race.

I remember going to Lewis' church and seeing people full of the Holy Ghost jumping and dancing around. As a kid I attended a more traditional, formal church, so I thought it was strange, but years later when I was filled with the Holy Spirit and had my own Pentecost, none of this seemed so strange to me, including speaking in tongues.

There was a particular time when Lewis' beliefs came in very handy for me. I was a freshman in college and had come down with mononucleosis, the so-called kissing disease. I had to come home. After I'd been home for a week or two Lewis came over to pray for me. (Mom told me later that Lewis mistakenly thought that I had a much more serious disease.) He laid his hands on me and prayed fervently. A day or two later I was back in college, and my strength rapidly returned.

Lewis was a role model for all of us as his brothers. When he died while in his sixties it left a big hole in our family. It hit dad the hardest because Lewis was his best friend. Unfortunately, Lewis and I didn't talk about race to any significant degree. Our age difference provided a kind of buffer for those kinds of conversations when I was growing up, and sadly he passed before I ever had a chance to discuss that with him as an adult.

Jim

My brother Jim set the tone for me personally. He left high school and joined the air force, where he got his GED and pursued two years of college. I remember that when he came home after his stint in the service I was so excited! Jim had the neatest cars, and he was just cool. He loved jazz and was well liked by everyone. He started working at the same Southern Wisconsin Center where Heddy worked with kids who had special needs. I remember Jim bringing one of them home for a weekend, and we played together. At that time I saw that my brother was tenderhearted, especially with anyone who was hurting or in need. That left a great impression on me.

From that first job, where he met his wife Patricia, Jim

moved on and became a loan officer at a bank in Milwaukee. Mom and Dad sold Jim and Patricia our house on St. Patrick Street, and my parents moved down the street to Charles Street. Jim was into cars, and as he prospered his cars got nicer. He taught me how to drive a stick shift with his Corvair. When I was in high school he also let me drive his Volkswagen Bug. When I was a senior he let me drive his Shelby GT 350. He was a true brother, taking me under his wing. He introduced me to Ugandan businessmen that he'd met, and I got to sit in my parents' living room and ask them questions about their country. This gave me a different perspective on life than I had known. Jim also had a house full of books. Like mom, he always read. He read everything! Even though he didn't finish college Jim was one of the most well read people I knew.

Jim must have been influenced by Lewis's entrepreneurial streak. I saw this firsthand when I lived with Jim and Pat in Milwaukee for a summer during my freshmen year of college. Jim had started his own nightclub, Alfie's. He would bring in various entertainers, and the place was always filled. At Alfie's I met Shirley MacLaine, Jim McMillian, who was a power forward for the Wilt Chamberlain–led Los Angeles Lakers, and other celebrities. He paid me to work for him that summer, and I was exposed to some really great music. My brother expanded my musical horizons beyond rock and roll to jazz.

From Alfie's, Jim worked for Miller Brewing Company and became an executive within their special events department. If there was a jazz fest, he had a hand in it. If Miller was at the Indy 500, he was there. He got to travel all over the country and beyond. He would share his experiences with me, and it helped to expand my view of how large my world could be and that my possibilities in life might be endless.

Jim and I talked quite a bit; he was candid about how the world worked. He told me that there was still a glass ceiling for blacks—it was just a little higher than it had been before. He made it clear that there was a topping-out for blacks that was different than for whites. He would tell me that in order to go higher as a black person you would have to be let into "the club." Whites and blacks, even at the highest levels, did not socialize beyond a certain point. There were country clubs that blacks couldn't belong to, or were not invited to, where the powerful played and made business connections. The Augusta National Country Club, where the Masters Tournament is held, is an example. For years Tiger Woods and a few other black golfers could play there, but they couldn't belong there.[3]

My brother told me about the conversations he'd had with blacks who'd made it to the level of vice president in their companies. They would tell him that they never really belonged. There were conversations that they needed to be a part of, but they occurred in the course of socializing outside of work, and since blacks were not a part of those conversations and relationships they couldn't network enough to get to the top of the mountain.

Jim's perspective weighed on me. I was an idealist and believed that the playing field was level. I believed our country was a meritocracy and that the old days of discrimination were over. This was the dawning of a new day! But Jim believed there was a more subtle reason for the limits of black success.

Jim is retired now, and we still discuss these issues out on the golf course, even though we're at opposite ends of the political spectrum. Whether it was intentional or not, my parents raised their sons to be independent thinkers, and Jim is one of my liberal brothers. He knows Jesse Jackson and other political luminaries personally. When we talk about politics we rarely agree, but I have noticed lately that we are moving closer toward the same views. We're beginning to agree that neither political party has an answer to the problems that this nation faces. Although he believes the Democrats have a better handle, I've reminded him that neither party really cares deeply about what is best for the common man. I believe there are only a few people in government that seem to place the best interest of the country ahead of their own. When you look at the fact that very little is done in Washington, DC, that really impacts the average American citizen it seems that we send people there only to be professional politicians. Whether they are Democrats or Republicans they seem to be the ruling elite. As a result I am becoming apolitical, not trusting many politicians and the promises that seem to so easily manipulate the voters.

ARZELL

My brother Arzell, whom we call Junior, is a full-time extrovert like our dad. He can talk to anyone. This was even evident when he was a child. Junior owned a shoe-shine kit when he was a pre-teen in the 1950s. He would set up shop outside of public businesses and make money by shining shoes. Dad loved it, and he jokingly called Junior a hustler.

His second job of note was at Meadowbrook Country Club, where he started as a caddie and later became an attendant in the men's room. This enabled him to buy his first car—a Chevy convertible—while still in high school.

As an elementary school kid I loved riding around in my brother's car. He said he would have stayed in that job at Meadowbrook, but he wanted to be more independent. Dad had rules about using a car, and if you broke his rules—even if you owned the car—he grounded you. When Junior broke a curfew rule (or something of that caliber) and Dad grounded him, it was the straw that broke the camel's back. Junior went off to the recruiter's office and enlisted in the air force. A few days later Dad drove Junior to Milwaukee so he could fly to Lackland Air Force Base with the other recruits. Junior told me that Dad gave him some money, bid him farewell, and watched him take off.

I find it funny that my brothers Jim and Junior joined the air force so that no one would tell them what to do. Dad's rules seemed really oppressive and controlling, but ironically, my brothers fled to an institution that told them when to get up, when to lie down, when to eat, what to eat, and when to go to the bathroom.

The air force made men out of my brothers and gave them the discipline they needed to become successful. If you go to either of their homes for a meal they instinctively pick up the dishes from the table and march off to the kitchen to wash them. It is that old air force training that's embedded in them.

Junior was stuck doing kitchen patrol (KP) while stationed at an air force base in Goose Bay in Labrador, Canada. One day when a captain was touring the barracks he stopped in Junior's room and noticed some of his drawings hanging on the wall. Junior was a gifted artist, and the captain was so impressed with his drawings that he pulled my brother out of KP duty and had him trained in the field of technical illustration. None of this was a surprise to the members of our family. Junior's artistic talent surfaced when he was very young. The fine arts director for the Racine Unified School District, Helen Patton, recognized one of Junior's third-grade landscape watercolors as exceptional, and she framed and hung it in her office for years. Eventually she gave it back, and my parents kept that framed painting on the wall of their home for the rest of their lives.

After eight years in the air force Junior was honorably discharged, and he went to work for a manufacturing business in Racine. The people he worked for were greatly impressed with his work, and Junior enjoyed the same kind of favor my dad did. People were predisposed toward him and helped him in his success. Eventually he moved to Denver, Colorado, to work for Marathon Oil as a technical illustrator.

Junior was moving up the ladder little by little, but then he hit a discrimination barrier when he was up for a promotion. Contrary to the advice of some, he filed a suit against the company for unfair practices. Though he won, he lost. As many of us know, suing the company that you work for is not the road to long-term opportunity. Junior eventually left, as the doors for him closed there. He turned to his artistic ability, including portraits and landscapes, as a means of support. He did a series of paintings on the Buffalo soldiers and other historical black figures and even created a portrait of singer Roberta Flack, which he presented to her. He has also done portraits of Duke Ellington and Bill Cosby over the years. He can paint ultra-modern impressionism as well as traditional styles of art. Some of his art has been displayed at the University of Alabama.

Currently he owns a graphic arts business in the Atlanta

area, and he has no desire to retire. He is always looking for new things to do and new worlds to explore. I think it's his contact with other people that fuels his desire to keep going.

Over the years Junior and I have talked about race on many occasions. He has shared some of the experiences that he and Jim had growing up. Since he is about nine years older than I am, our experiences are different. The 1960s civil rights movement reached its zenith when he was a young adult and I was still a child. He and Jim experienced discrimination head on—without the benefit of legislative remedies and changes in culture taking hold—when they were starting out as young adults. While my younger brother, Stan, and I were able to go to college and receive great educations, Junior and Jim were given a slow start in southern schools. Their experience of having to work doubly hard to overcome that inertia stands in stark contrast to the kind of momentum they could have had if they had been born in the North.

Some of the experiences that are recorded in this book are ones that Junior shared with me from his life. Junior is a go-getter and has served as a great role model. With his example I have been less afraid to venture out and explore new vistas. Through Junior I have learned that being persistent is one of the keys to success. If one door closes, find another one. If opportunity closes down in one part of the country, move to another. I have also found that being open and friendly with people has its advantages over the course of a lifetime. Dad taught us that, and Junior has continued his legacy.

Junior is the other liberal Democrat among my brothers, even painting pictures and producing T-shirts with President Obama's picture on them. He believes the answer to a lot of the woes for blacks lies more in their affiliation with the Democrats than the Republicans. Because we live so far apart we don't engage in the same banter that Jim and I do. Every once in a while we talk politics, and most of the time we agree to disagree.

STAN

My brother Stan is the youngest. As I mentioned earlier, Stan was so light-skinned when he was born that they printed "white" on his birth certificate. Stan is three and one-half years younger than I am. I remember being jealous of him when he was born. Up until then I was the baby of the family, with dark, curly hair. People fawned over me, but then along came this curly, sandy-haired child, and suddenly people treated me like the ugly duckling. In time I got over that, and as we grew up together, Stan became my best friend. My brother was an excellent student and an exceptional athlete, becoming a champion gymnast at the high school and collegiate levels. As a result Stan won a scholarship to Wheaton College in Illinois. I enjoyed visiting him when he was there.

Stan experienced some of the same rejections that I did due to his race. When you grow up with people of different races it never occurs to you that you can't date them or they you. The times, they were a changing—or so we thought. It was the late seventies when Stan wanted to date a white girl he really cared about. She was a Christian, and so were her parents, but they did not want them to date. She was deeply hurt by her parent's prejudice, and I remember the pain this caused Stan as well. He moved on and did not let things stop him, though it hurt. Rejection is never a mere scrape of the knee. It can leave a deeper wound if you let it.

Stan went on to do very well at Wheaton, where he excelled in academics and sports. I was so proud of how well he did, though his success was never a surprise to me. He also met his first wife, Melodie, at Wheaton. After college Stan started his career as a teacher, moving out to Great Bend, Kansas, near Sterling, Kansas, where Peggy and I lived. After a few years he relocated to work at a private academy on Long Island. While on the East Coast he received his master's degree from Harvard in educational administration.

With his degree, Stan moved back home to Racine and became a top young administrator. We talked about the limitations that racial prejudice could have on his future career, and although he had the potential to keep advancing I think he realized his opportunities might be limited in Wisconsin. Stan and Melodie moved back to the East Coast, where there were more blacks in prominent places of leadership in education.

Over the years Stan has been the principal of Newport High School in Rhode Island, headmaster of Times² Academy in Providence, and part of Ted Sizer's Coalition of Essential Schools. He has also been a leader in applied educational reform. Currently Stan works for a foundation on the East Coast. He has put together an exceptional career, and I have always been proud of him. In fact, I am proud of all my brothers, as you can see. They have served as role models for me and pioneers who laid a path for me to follow. They have inspired me and honored the sacrifices of my parents to build successful lives.

My son, Nate, talks about his uncles all the time. When he was young he would go on vacations with Jim and his son Jimmy in their RV. Nate got to travel to places that we couldn't take him. Uncle Jim was more prosperous and went to interesting places. Through him, Nate saw what might be possible if you were smart and resourceful.

I have always wondered which of my parents had the greater impact on the success of my brothers and myself. Was it my mother or my father? I don't mean a superficial success as the world defines it, branded by money, fame, and prestige. This kind of success is the ability to be men of solid faith and character, derived from a real relationship with God. This may seem like a silly question to ask. Most of us assume that we get a little bit of our success from both of our parents, inheriting some of their strengths and weaknesses. They give us our initial pair of lenses through which we view the world until we develop our own.

For the longest time I thought my mother was the X factor because of her education and aspirations to achieve. Peggy reminded me, however, that it was my father who was the real go-getter. Mom tended to be conservative and frugal. She took risks, but only calculated ones. Dad, on the other hand, would take the kind of risks that pushed the family farther ahead. He was more of a spender and would make the key decisions that opened greater opportunities for the family. My dad only had a third-grade education, but I think that weighed on us all, and it inspired us to want more for ourselves. We knew that Dad was a bright guy, especially when it came to the psychology of human beings. I always felt badly that he didn't have the chance to combine a good education with his other positive attributes, but my brothers and I have our parents to thank for our love of learning.

In time my father's influence in my life would transcend the values of hard work and just being a good man, and he would have a great influence on my faith as an adult. I have already mentioned how my mother instilled in me a love for the Bible from the time I was a child. My dad was not a part of that. He was a heavy drinker during those days and was riding on the coattails of Mom's faith. When I met Christ during my junior year of college one of the first people I shared my newfound faith with was my dad. He immediately gave his life to Jesus and was instantly set free from his lifelong addiction to alcohol. From that point our relationship changed. Some years later, when I pastored a church in Racine, my father and mother joined the fellowship. Each Sunday they would be there to support my ministry. In hard times it was my dad's prayers that encouraged me and carried me through. Eventually it was the faith and example of hard work of both of my parents that proved to be the X factor in my life.

One of my most precious memories is when my father, like an Old Testament patriarch, passed his blessing on to his sons. About a month before he died my father spoke very directly and deliberately to my brother Jim and me while we were visiting him in the hospital one day.

"You know," he said, "I was always used to carrying money in my pocket. It made me feel good. But now at the end money doesn't mean anything to me." His words were slow, steady, and impacting.

"I want the two of you to know how proud I am of the men that you have become," he continued. "I am also proud of your other brothers." (Junior and Stan lived out of state and weren't able to be there at the time.)

As I reflected on that moment I realized my dad was making peace with his children and leaving behind a priceless inheritance. There are many parents who pass away without ever telling their children how much they love them or how proud they are of them. This leaves a lifelong emptiness in their children's lives, but my dad helped to establish a security in me that has helped me in the years since. Beyond a shadow of a doubt, I know that he loved us and he was proud of us. What a great legacy!

Chapter 14
JUSTICE AND THE LENS OF RACE

H ANDS UP. DON'T *shoot. I can't breathe.*
Unless you've been living under a rock, you likely recognize these words as powerful symbols of racial conflict in America. From the I Am a Man! mantra of the civil rights protests in the 1960s to the Black Lives Matter cries of today, racism is a gift that keeps on giving.

When I first began writing this book there was very little media attention given to the militarization of police and racial profiling. Within a year the 2014 rioting in Ferguson, Missouri, lifted the veil from America's eyes regarding both. Today, the growing reports of young, unarmed black men being shot to death when stopped by police is astounding. Others died from abuse or neglect while in police custody. While many argue that these young men would be alive if they had simply not resisted arrest, I agree with this only to a point. The question is, If a suspect is unarmed, why not use an alternate form of restraint, such as tasers?

Although my parents were law-abiding citizens and raised me as such, I have to admit that I have always had a kind of paranoia where the police are concerned. I don't say this to incite any anger or rebellion toward the authorities but rather to share my own experiences and apprehension. If I'm driving down the street and a police officer is behind me, I develop some anxiety, even when I know I'm going slower than the speed limit. Maybe everyone feels this way, but I have been pulled over before without cause. Recently, as I was driving on a northern Wisconsin interstate highway I passed a state patrol car. A moment later I cringed as I noticed that he was following me with his lights flashing.

"Why is he following me?" I wondered. "I'm doing the speed limit."

Carefully pulling over, I kept my hands on the steering wheel, reluctant to reach for my wallet or vehicle registration. I held my breath and waited, uncertain of what would happen as the officer approached my window.

"Are you aware that your lights are not on and it's dusk?" he asked, without asking for identification.

"No sir," I responded. "Thank you."

As I breathed a sigh of relief he reached into the car and patted me on the back. The fact that he was Hispanic made me feel somewhat relaxed. I felt that he might have understood my anxiety, having maybe experienced something similar at some point in his life.

Over the years I've read of similar experiences that have occurred with black men, including professionals, who were shot after reaching for their vehicle registrations after being pulled over for traffic violations. In some instances the officer took an approach beyond caution, expecting a confrontation or presuming that the person had criminal intent. As a result I have counseled my own sons for years that if a police officer pulls them over, do not, for any reason, reach into the glove box for their ID without first receiving the officer's permission, and under absolutely no circumstance reach for their wallet or anything else. This sounds eerily similar to the advice my parents gave to my brothers and me before traveling to the Jim Crow South when we were kids. I wonder if white parents have to give this type of survival advice to their children.

As a black man with a white wife, a black (adopted) son, and three (biological) mixed-race sons I have tried to refuse to filter the world through the lens of race, but at times I find it unavoidable. Despite the social changes we've seen, the perceptions that feed America's race-related headlines today are the same ones that inflamed past conflicts in our nation, and the protests and repercussions that follow lead me to examine the differences between how blacks and whites view the government and court system, and particularly the police.

Among the well-known charges of racial injustice is the account of a black immigrant Amadou Diallo, as recorded in Malcolm Gladwell's book *Blink*. It's the story of an unarmed black man who was shot in 1999 by New York City police officers. When police confronted him asking what he was doing in front of an apartment building where he lived, he reached into his vest pocket for his wallet. The police officers responded by firing forty-one bullets, with nineteen striking his body, killing him. The officers later claimed that he looked like a rape suspect that they were looking for. Tragically, they had killed a twenty-two-year-old West African immigrant with no criminal record. Although this case prompted a huge public outcry, the officers were exonerated, making this one of the most blatant examples of why even educated, middle- and upper-class black people have what some would consider an irrational fear of police.

A friend of mine who is biracial told me about an experience she had as a child that still affects her emotionally. When she was eight years old, in the late 1980s, her family was standing outside of their house. All of a sudden police officers appeared. They came up to her father, who was black, and grabbed him, shoving him to the ground. They pushed his face into the ground. She was crying, along with her mother and sister. When the officers put him into the police car and called in his name they discovered that they had the wrong man! They were looking for a black robbery suspect. All of this happened to an educated, middle-class black man who was trying to raise his children to respect the law. My friend is now a teacher, and she tells me that she still reacts when police are around.

In 1991 a black man was pulled over by police in Los Angeles, taken out of his car, and told to get to the ground. He was then beaten repeatedly by white police officers. The Rodney King incident drew national attention when someone videotaped the beating, not unlike the outrage over the shooting of Michael Brown in Ferguson, Missouri.

Let me say up front that I believe Rodney King was guilty. He was high on drugs, and his refusal to get on the ground and allow police officers to handcuff him put him in jeopardy. But the contentious debates about his case and others reveal the differences between the perceptions of whites and blacks. The beating of King by police officers was par for the course to many blacks. While they were shocked by the brutality, they were not surprised by it. Whites focused on his lawlessness in not complying with the police and his being high on drugs as justification for the actions of the police. Blacks saw it as another straw on the black camel's back. The court case was so inflammatory that the trial was moved to Simi Valley, a community where the majority of the population and jury were white.

When the police officers were exonerated the worst fears of both whites and blacks were realized. There were horrible riots. Store after store was burned in sections of Los Angeles. One particular poignant story was of a white truck driver, Reginald Denny, who was pulled from his truck and severely beaten while driving through the area. If not for the goodwill of some of the black residents who protected him, he would have been a fatal casualty of racial hatred.

A few days later the *Nightline* news show held a town hall meeting with an audience of both whites and blacks who were also diverse socioeconomically and professionally. I watched the discussion with rapt attention, amazed at the completely different perspectives the audience had, split along racial lines. The argument was vehement and filled with emotion, and while Ted Koppel tried his best to moderate, he had his hands full. Race is not a just a topic to be discussed dispassionately to many blacks. It is not a philosophical or sociological dialogue. It is the opening of wounds, personal and historical. The Rodney King incident reminded older blacks of the lynching of Emmett Till or of instance after instance of mistreatment of themselves or family members.

As an example, one of my nieces shared some interesting perceptions with me right after the 1995 murder trial of actor and Hall of Fame running back O J Simpson. As a black man his marriage to a white woman, Nicole Brown, brought him into disfavor with a number of other black people, and it didn't change after they divorced either. To some, he was still an outcast for having married a white woman.

The facts of the case are well-known. He was accused of murdering Nicole and a young man, Ron Goldman. As the case played out in the news, people formed opinions about his guilt or innocence. I can still see O J clumsily trying to put on the murderer's gloves and how poorly they fit. This was seen as proof that he could not be the murderer. But I had my own opinions about O J's guilt and felt strongly that because he had money, he escaped his punishment. Robert Shapiro told interviewer Barbara Walters, "Not only did we play the race card, we dealt it from the bottom of the deck."[1]

A few days after the conclusion of the trial I saw my niece in the parking lot of a grocery store. We talked about family things first, just catching up. Then our conversation turned to the O J Simpson case.

"What did you think of the verdict?" I asked.

"I'm glad he got off," she answered.

I was shocked. I thought he was guilty as sin, and I wondered how she could be so easily manipulated by the defense. She then said something that is consistent with my premise that race is a complex issue because it wanders into other areas of discussion.

"Black people rarely get a fair shake from the criminal justice system," she explained. In her mind, O J's guilt or innocence was of secondary importance to the overall issue of justice for black people. In her opinion this was simply a balancing of the scales back toward justice.

Over the next number of days focus groups of people— both black and white—were polled, and not surprisingly, their opinions almost always skewed along racial lines, with whites overwhelmingly thinking he was guilty and blacks saying he was innocent, or at the very least that he was a victim of a justice system that had it in for black men.

What is the role of the church in any of these situations? you may ask. First, we are always aware of the fact that human beings are flawed and fall short of God's purposes and standards. This includes governments and those who enforce the law. Though each situation is unique and complex, as ambassadors of Christ we are called to reach out to the lost. The church must learn to speak up as one voice, especially against injustice. This is not a time to recoil into our black and white comfort zones. Rather, it's an opportunity for the segregated church to come together to ask questions and seek justice in unity.

It's a difficult path to walk because Christians tend to follow the law without any questions about how it is being executed. This is partly why the church was slow to respond to the injustice perpetrated against blacks in the South for many decades following the Civil War. This helped to reinforce segregation in the church because black Christians questioned whether white Christians would apply the love of Christ to alleviate the suffering they were experiencing.

Jesus said, "Render therefore to Caesar the things that are Caesar's, and to God the things that are God's" (Matthew 22:21, NKJV). Keep in mind, though, that the Bible does allow for Christians to question the law when it violates an even higher law. As Peter said in Acts 5:29, "We ought to obey God rather than men" (NKJV). We may respond to this truth during times of persecution when injustice is obvious, but the escalating racial conflicts are shining a light on many assumptions we've made about civil disobedience. Although the gospel is about personal transformation, the church can be a powerful redemptive force when it manifests the kingdom of God on a massive level. Those who truly live out the gospel can become a voice of reason to calm the emotions that so easily flare up and cause hatred and violence. When we cry out for justice we do so from the eyes of God. And when we respond with mercy and forgiveness it is transformative.

Jesus said the church is to be salt and light in the world. (See Matthew 5:13–16.) You don't need salt if something is not tending toward corruption and decay if left to itself.

The presence of light presumes that there is darkness that needs to be chased away. The belief that all police are racist or corrupt has to be confronted by the church. It is not true. The corollary, however, that all actions of the police and government are always right must also be questioned.

There are people in society who have used injustice as permission to harm police and disobey civil authority, which has led to the shooting of police. The church needs to decry this kind of action at all times. Since we are not of this world, we have a unique perspective to speak to this society. The Bible says we are "aliens and strangers" (1 Pet. 2:11, AMP), and consequently we are to judge things from a kingdom perspective and not from our political or social frameworks.

Neither are we to view race strictly politically through a liberal or conservative lens. We are not forced to choose from the lesser of two evils when trying to find solutions to human problems. We have the wisdom of a God who sees all sides of an issue and has solutions that defy conventional thinking. What would it be like for the world to see the church as a group of people who, like Jesus, had supernatural influence without being conformed to its way of thinking? We could model a different way of confronting injustice and helping ensure that some of the root causes are not allowed to continue and fester.

Didn't Jesus tell us in Matthew 6:10 to pray, "Your kingdom come, your will be done, on earth as it is in heaven" (NKJV)? The kingdom is not to be demonstrated through the world but through the church to the world. The divisiveness of race provides one of the greatest opportunities to demonstrate the kingdom of God.

Chapter 15
PROGRESS AND THE
UNFINISHED WORK

I HAVE LIVED THROUGH a time when there were few black athletes in professional sports and few black coaches. We have progressed from the first black quarterback in the playoffs in 1974, James Harris, to the first to win a Super Bowl in 1988, Doug Williams. From that we moved to the first Super Bowl with two black coaches, Lovie Smith and Tony Dungy, leading their opposing teams in 2006.

All of these things, along with the strides we've made in politics by electing our first black president in 2008, show a good history of progress, and I have no desire to minimize them. I have lived through a good portion of the important transitions in race relationships in this country, and I've been the beneficiary of these changes and the opportunities that they have created for me. When it comes to the subject and experience of race many blacks would like to move on and live out what Martin Luther King Jr. talked about in his "I Have A Dream" speech. He longed for a time when his children would not be judged "by the color of their skin, but by the content of their character."[1] Although we are moving closer to that goal there is still a need to keep building on past progress.

If I told you my high school mascot was a short, squatty Confederate officer dressed in his gray uniform and the school flag was the Confederate flag you'd likely assume I attended school in the South. But my alma mater is

William Horlick High School, the home of the Rebels, in Racine, Wisconsin.

Although I wasn't very athletic I loved sports, so I tried out for football as a sophomore. One day after practice I turned to one of my friends, who also was black, and I announced to him that before we graduated I was going to change the Horlick flag. By this time significant events were happening in this country. Voting rights were a reality, and blacks were beginning to realize their first taste of the promises of the American dream. Progress was exceedingly slow, but it was still progress, and I'd been motivated by Dr. Martin Luther King Jr. and others who'd fought racism.

I bided my time and waited. I didn't become a superstar athlete or one of the most popular kids in school, but over time I was well-known enough to feel like I had a voice that people might listen to. I approached our new principal with confidence.

"Mr. Stenavich," I said, "I want to speak to you about something that is very important to me." He was sympathetic and invited me to sit down and encouraged me to continue talking.

"What's on your mind?" he asked.

"Mr. Stenavich," I continued, "from my sophomore year I have been really troubled by the fact that our school flag is the Confederate flag. The Confederate flag is the same as the swastika; it is a symbol of hatred. It has troubled me up to this point, and I have been thinking that it's time for the flag to be changed. Given all of the change that's going on in the country I thought that I would approach you now."

To his credit, he listened to me patiently. "I understand how you feel," he said, "but I can't make the decision to make the change unilaterally." There was a lot of history, and some of the alumni would be upset if he made that decision. He pondered it for a moment.

"I have an idea," he continued. "We can sponsor an art contest allowing students to present designs for a new Horlick flag. This would be the first step, and then we would choose five designs and then allow students to vote for a reasonable replacement to the Confederate flag."

I was apprehensive about the plan. I wasn't sure that I trusted my classmates to come to the right decision, but I conceded because I figured in a democracy you have to take your chances, trusting people's consciences to come to the right conclusions. The principal also gave students the option of keeping the present flag, a choice that I didn't understand at all at the time. Back then I was really naïve; I thought if you presented people with the truth and trusted them they would make the right choice. Later, through studying history in college, I learned the folly of that belief.

Some really amazing things happened during what I now refer to as the flag fight. First, I almost got into a fist-fight with one of my best friends. He was black and was wondering why I was stirring up such a fuss. When I told him why he shoved me up against a locker, and only the intervention of other people kept me from getting beat up. Other friends I'd known from childhood told me that they hated me. It was about the most isolated and lonely feeling that I had ever experienced to that point in my life. I didn't know that standing up for principle was so costly. Oddly, I didn't talk to my parents about any of this. I don't know why. If anyone would have understood how I felt it would have been my mom and dad. They would have also understood why it was important for me to take this stand.

The various designs were whittled down to five choices. I thought there were some exceptional designs that kept the school colors of scarlet and gray and the concept of the school's previous nickname, the North Stars. In fact, the yearbook was named *Polaris* after the North Star. When the students voted, one design rose to the top, but it wasn't more popular than the original flag. This was 1971, and the old flag prevailed—a defeat I would just have to live with. But I was so angry about the choice of keeping the Confederate flag that I refused to have my picture taken for the yearbook (a decision that I now regret). I didn't want to identify with that symbol in any way, and that seemed like the only way I could protest the decision about the flag at that time.

A few years later when I was home from college I attended a basketball game at Horlick. I took my seat in the bleachers and dreaded looking up on the wall where the flag hung. I did not want to have to view that symbol of hatred and oppression mocking me for my failed attempt to remove it. But when I looked up I almost fell off of the bleachers. The Confederate flag was gone! In its place was one of the designs I recognized from the contest. I felt an overwhelming sense of relief and some degree of vindication. I hadn't been the valedictorian or a state-recognized athlete, but maybe I'd left a mark after all.

In college I majored in history and education, and my high school also became the launching point for my career in education. When Mr. Stenavich hired me as a human relations advisor at Horlick in 1975 he told me how the flag had changed. He had kept the designs from the contest, and after a few years as the national conscience moved forward he decided it was time for the old Confederate flag to go. There was no justification for keeping it any longer.

This experience taught me the value of timing and the biblical precept of sowing and reaping when it comes to change. It also taught me how to stand up for a cause I believed in, even if it cost me friendships. God delights in taking some of the areas of our greatest defeats and shame and turning them around. Scripture promises that God will restore to us the years that the locust have eaten away (Joel 2:25), and that He will cause all things to work together for our good (Rom. 8:28). For me, a complete healing process and restoration took place. The hurt and resentment I'd carried since my senior year began to lift. In time I started attending class reunions and began looking forward to seeing my classmates. The restoration was made complete when some of them nominated me for the Distinguished Alumni Award in 2013. I received the award—a great honor bestowed on only a few of the graduates of my high school. It was an emotional occasion for me at the recognition ceremony, completely burying the hurt of the past.

Though many years have passed since the Horlick flag was changed, the Confederate flag has survived throughout our land. Through the 1970s and beyond it flew over the state houses of southern states in one form or another. Though politicians would come up with a rationale for why they could not take the flag down, it became a constant stain upon the national conscience. As a reminder of past injustices, to many it casts a dark shadow over all the progress of the last fifty years. While some see it as a symbol of southern pride, others can't overlook the implications of slavery that it proclaims. As with many changes, it took a tragedy to cause southern politicians to say, "Enough is enough!"

Some of the worst atrocities of the civil rights period

were committed against people who were in houses of worship. Churches were bombed, and children died. It is not completely surprising, then, that it would take a tragedy in a church with innocent worshipers to show the horror of racism yet again. In 2015 nine black church members were shot dead at Emanuel African Methodist Episcopal Church in Charleston, South Carolina, by a man who said his intent was to start a race war. The shock to the nation was palpable as the debate about the Confederate flag flared up again. But this time there was a change. Instead of the same rhetoric, which had rationalized some of the same racial hatred that had been embedded in the South, different voices were being heard, especially through the victims' families.

The families of those who were killed did not cry out for vengeance but instead offered forgiveness and mercy. This was a sharp contrast to the riots that many expected, and the reaction of the news media and commentators was a testimony to the power of the gospel when demonstrated by love. Many said they had never seen that kind of forgiveness. It started the process necessary to remove the Confederate flag as a symbol from several state governments.

Nikki Haley, the governor of South Carolina, stepped forward and said the Confederate flag had to go. Signing a bill to remove the flag from the state capitol led to a widespread movement to withdraw or even stop selling it in other places nationwide. There was no justification for keeping the flag, no argument to maintain the flag in the name of preserving a part of southern history and tradition.

Months later, Peggy and I attended a conference in South Carolina at a church pastored by Mahesh Chavda.

During the conference we became acquainted with a couple from the Charleston area. They told us that a few weeks before the shooting at Mother Emanuel, a very large group of blacks and whites gathered together to seek God for revival, praying fervently and on their knees together. Governor Haley and Louisiana governor Bobby Jindal, both of Indian-American descent, were there. But they were not there to campaign; instead they shared their testimonies and they prayed. This provided a spiritual backdrop for the change that was going to happen. It helped us to understand that even though an evil man was motivated to spew hatred, God was not caught off guard and was mobilizing His army beforehand to demonstrate love.

Although our nation has made progress regarding race, today many people have grown weary of the topic. Some say racial issues have gone away, arguing that the effect of legal discrimination and racism has dissipated over time. But remnants of racism and discrimination remain. Some are overt, others are subtle, yet they have damaging, long-lasting results, and getting people to buy in to the need for change is still a struggle.

Some believe that landmark court cases and legislation, including affirmative action to remedy past wrongs, have eliminated the need to focus on the long-term effects of racism. I wish this were true, but racism has had a lasting effect on educational opportunities and the wealth gap between whites and blacks. The fact that efforts toward fair housing and education are relatively recent innovations accruing benefits primarily to the current generation also escapes notice.

Many studies have been done on the role of race in the wealth gap in our country. One thought-provoking story was a PBS special called *Race: The Power of an Illusion.*

I was impressed by one segment that discussed how race continues to impact the lives of black people unlike any other ethnic group. The segment "A Tale of Two Families" showed the disparity between long-term opportunities between blacks and whites.[2] The story is really about the two directors of the company responsible for making the *Race: The Power of an Illusion* series: Byron, who is black, and Max, who is white. Both are about the same age, and because they work for the same company they make the same income, but that does not make their lives similar. To examine this, we must go back one generation to their parents.

In the 1950s Byron's parents bought a two-story duplex in one of the areas of Chester, Pennsylvania, that would rent to blacks. The home sold for $6,500 dollars. At about the same time Max's parents married, and with a combination of money from his parents and a government VA loan they bought a home in a new, white suburban development on Long Island, New York. It was a $21,500 home in 1952. Byron's dad found a job as a laboratory assistant, and his mom worked as a domestic for white families in the suburbs. Max's dad got a college education through the GI Bill. Though blacks also had access to the GI Bill, discrimination in university admission and also in housing for blacks limited the opportunities of the heroes returning from the Second World War. After graduation he started as a management trainee and worked for a textile firm for fifteen years.

The economy in Chester became depressed, and housing remained segregated. Taxes continued to go up as things got worse. Max's family experienced higher property values since they were in a wealthy area with better infrastructure. In this environment Max's dad started his own business by tapping into his home's equity. His business did so well that in time he sent all three of his children, including Max, to private colleges.

Byron also went to an Ivy League school on an academic scholarship. Whereas Byron struggled to save every penny that he could, Max began accumulating wealth with money from his bar mitzvah. He used that money, along with funds from his parents, to travel and to go to college without having to worry about finances.

In time both Max's and Byron's parents sold their homes. By the late nineties Chester's population was 76 percent black, and Byron's parents sold their home for $29,500, about four and a half times what they paid for it, which did not provide much of a nest egg for their retirement. Conversely, Max's parents sold their home for $299,000, about fourteen times what they paid for it. They retired to the Berkshire Mountains and helped their children with down payments on their own homes.

Byron looks after his parents' finances, helping them from time to time. Max bought his own home in 1985 with money from his parents; his home is all paid for, and he lives financially secure. He is able to pass on his wealth to his children, a portion of which is what his parents passed on to him.

I shared this story with my son, Matt, to drive home the point that there is no meritocracy. If you're growing up racially segregated because of where you live, your experience of America isn't like the rest of America. Max's parents were not any smarter, hard working, or deserving than Byron's, whose skin color provided a pathway to certain opportunities (the GI Bill, living in a developing suburb, and receiving intergenerational wealth). Property wealth is one of the ways that families build wealth, but discrimination impairs the ability for some people to do so by restricting them to the ghetto or to inferior schools. This lag effect of wealth is still affecting many black families.

Some whites would argue that they didn't grow up rich or lacked the opportunity that Max and his family had. That may be true, but I would point to the fact that blacks have been hindered from wealth by legal and intentional discrimination for generations. If you were white you might pull yourself up by your own bootstraps; legal discrimination did not stand in your way. If you were black for the longest time it did not matter how strong or long your bootstraps were or how hard you pulled on them. Institutional racism was a limiting factor that you couldn't get around. Until there is a completely level playing field and the only difference is based on initiative, there remains work to be done.

So what happens to those who have pulled themselves up by their bootstraps? What about those who have won acclaim and widespread celebrity? Do they escape the embarrassment and degradation of experiencing discrimination?

An ABC special that aired in the late nineties did a story on Danny Glover, an actor of some fame and recognition. His starring role in the *Lethal Weapon* movies and others made him a high profile and recognizable character. With cameras filming, he tried to hail a taxicab in New York City, but in one day five passed him and refused to stop. Believing it was because he is black, Glover said, "I don't expect to have a taxi. I've been conditioned to think that someone is not going to stop for me."[3] Though he assumed he was recognized, being rich and famous did not spare him the indignity that many lesser-profile blacks had to endure as their normal life experience. Whether or not the taxi drivers recognized him, the question remains, How can a black man combat the stereotypes that follow him?

A decade later *Good Morning America* wanted to see if things had changed, so they did a similar experiment with Christopher Darden, a black attorney in the O J case, and a white man of about the same age, forty-one years old.[4] As the two men stood on the sidewalk attempting to hail a cab during the daytime hours, taxi drivers did not hesitate to pick either of them up. However, this changed when the night came. Taxis would pick up the white man without any hesitation, but Mr. Darden was not as lucky. Cabs would slow down to look at him, notice that he was black, and then flip on the light that indicated that they were already occupied. Were these drivers reluctant to deliver their clients to high-crime black neighborhoods after dark? Or did they believe that black men are more dangerous than white men?

After a 2014 interview, Mark Cuban, the owner of the Dallas Mavericks, suffered greatly in the media for publicly saying what many people think: "If I see a black kid in a hoodie, and it's late at night, I'm walking to the other side of the street."[5] Mark Cuban is not a racist, but there are many people who operate out of the belief that blacks, especially black men, are potentially dangerous.

To his defense, Cuban admitted that he also held other stereotypes. He continued, "If on that side of the street there's a guy that has tattoos all over his face—white guy, bald head, tattoos everywhere—I'm walking back to the other side of the street. And the list goes on of stereotypes that we all live up to and are fearful of…I think that helping people improve their lives, helping people engage with people they may fear or not understand, and helping people realize that while we all may have our prejudices and bigotries, we have to learn that it's an issue that we have to control."[6]

Chapter 16
OUT OF CHARACTER

As a child I developed a real sense of moral indignation toward discrimination and prejudice. I remember reading stories about apartheid in South Africa and wondering how anyone could be so hateful. Whether it was Fredrick Douglass or Martin Luther King Jr., I think blacks have, for the most part, shown incredible restraint in situations where they were being unequally treated. And as a Christian I am always trying to balance the need for change with the desire to exhibit godly character. This is never easy.

For years I just tolerated discrimination in my own life. I believed in things like the American dream and that all men are created equal. I also believed that if I worked hard enough and played by all of the rules I could climb the ladder of success and not experience the impediments of racism. My parents had experienced a lifetime of discrimination, but in spite of this they refused to allow my brothers and me to feel like victims just because we were black. After I became a Christian I came to believe that there were times I would just have to put up with things, whether they were right or wrong. I also knew that I had a God who helped me through my troubles and caused many of those obstacles to ultimately work out for my good, as is written in Romans 8:28.

My belief in passivity ultimately came to a head. I felt the exasperation and frustration that many other blacks feel when their frame of reference is misunderstood. Many blacks feel like they're living under a microscope, knowing they will have to live by a different standard than the people around them. Blacks who move into a primarily white neighborhood may feel like they have to keep their property at the highest standard or make an extra effort to be friendly. As a result of this additional scrutiny they may seem distant, untrusting, and even a little paranoid.

In 2008 during the presidential election Peggy and I went to vote in our new neighborhood in Kenosha, Wisconsin. We were the only black family in that part of the comfortable, middle-class subdivision. Entering the school, we saw people lining the hallways; the turnout was huge. As we walked toward the gym where the voting machines were I was focused on getting in, voting, and getting out.

"Did you notice that?" Peggy asked me afterward.

"Notice what?" I responded. I was clueless, but her antennae are always up.

"From the moment you walked through the door until you left," she said, "people were staring at you as if you were in the wrong polling place. I can't believe you didn't notice!"

Maybe my clothes were outdated or I had food on my face, but something tells me it was my race. And when I revisit memories like this, it reinforces the feeling of being a second-class citizen. I am an American. Being scrutinized while voting a few blocks from my home seems to relegate me to a shadowy place.

I also believe racial discrimination played a role in my termination from a superintendent position. During my employment I was careful to document all my vacation time and comp hours, including how I apportioned my time during conferences, in the event that it would ever come into question. Almost prophetically, the day came when I was accused of misusing vacation time, but when I was not asked to submit any proof to the contrary I was disappointed but not surprised. On occasions when I had left early on Fridays I'd asked my administrative assistant to mark it as vacation time, even if I'd already worked sufficient hours during the week. I later learned that it was common for one of my predecessors to leave early on Fridays without using vacation time, and no one questioned it. Why was I held to a different standard?

There were other restrictions put upon me that, in hindsight, felt like a trap. For example, I was instructed *not* to use work time to make notes about my work-related activities, meetings, and conversations. These were reference points for me in case I needed to report about them or recall a conversation. At a later date when my employment status was being reviewed, ironically I was asked to provide some notes about a meeting I attended. Fortunately I had asked my assistant to attend this evening meeting to take notes.

Although my performance began to be questioned by a few individuals I was prohibited from surveying the hundreds of teachers and staff to see how effective my leadership was. Soon the school board began meeting in closed session to discuss my tenure. Rumors about "administrative changes" began to swirl, and I was directed to keep silent. I learned that the school board hired an attorney, but nobody was forthright about the allegations against me. You can imagine how isolated I felt. Like David in the Book of Psalms, I was in a "slippery place" and felt that there were those who wanted me to stumble and fall. (See Psalm 73:18.)

Peggy knew the incredible turmoil I was going through

at work carrying on with business as usual day to day, all the while the sword of Damocles hanging over my head. She encouraged me to secure legal counsel, but this was out of character for me. As a conservative I had vowed never to file a lawsuit. I have always believed that many lawsuits are frivolous, and those that illegitimately play the race card only feed the *boy who cried wolf* affect. But my career was in jeopardy, and I had serious doubts that I would ever be rehired if I was terminated.

The moment I decided to stand up for myself a sense of peace came over me. It felt good not to let people walk over me; treating a person differently because you have the power to do so is just wrong. This didn't mean I would live in anger or bitterness, but Scripture speaks much about justice. God hates injustice, and sometimes when we allow wickedness to perpetuate, we become complicit with it.

There are several examples from the life of the apostle Paul in which he exerted his rights. In Acts 16:31–40 Paul and his companion, Silas, were beaten unjustly. When the chief magistrates tried to let him out of the jail quietly Paul said they had violated their rights by beating them and throwing them in jail without benefit of a trial. The magistrates were afraid when Paul told them that he was a Roman citizen, and they came and appealed to Paul and Silas, begging them to leave the city.

In Acts 22, on another occasion, Paul was about to be beaten because of an uproar that occurred after preaching the gospel. The Roman commander brought Paul into the barracks and ordered that he should be interrogated and scourged. When they had stretched him out and were about to put the lash to him Paul asserted his rights, asking, "Is it lawful for you to scourge a man who is a Roman and uncondemned?" (v. 25, NAS). Once again the

Roman commander was afraid because he violated Paul's rights.

Later, in Acts 23 the Jewish rulers were conspiring to kill Paul if he was going to have his case heard in Jerusalem. Paul found out about it, and then instead of allowing himself to be placed in their trap he exercised his right as a Roman citizen to appeal his case to Caesar.

In the midst of my own circumstances there were many townspeople who approached me to tell me what a wonderful job I was doing. I thanked them, knowing they were oblivious to all the secret wrangling that was going on. When God's blessing increases while life seems to be falling apart I call it being on the teeter-totter.

This happened to Joseph in the Bible. He was a rich kid who was unjustly sold into slavery by his jealous older brothers. Though a slave in a foreign land, he prospered in everything that he did. Even when he was falsely accused of seducing his master's wife and put into prison, the favor and blessing of God was all over him there, and he continued to prosper. Finally God brought about the circumstances that not only led to his release, but he was promoted to the place of second in command in the most powerful nation on Earth at that time, Egypt. Yep, it's the teeter-totter effect.

As I prepared to meet with an attorney I made a list of fifteen examples of treatment I endured that differed from my predecessors. I wondered if I should bring action for discrimination, so I conferred with an employment attorney who specialized in cases regarding superintendent contracts. I admitted to my failures in two of the numerous allegations against me, but he agreed that they alone wouldn't have been grounds for dismissal. The attorney—a white man—suspected discrimination and referred me to a civil rights attorney.

I thought it would be easy to sue for discrimination, but the civil rights attorney gave me a history lesson of the last few decades and how discrimination lawsuits work. I thought it would have been even easier to sue for discrimination in the 1960s and seventies, but he said it would have been much harder. "In the sixties and seventies," he said, "you had to prove overt, intentional racism." He made it clear that someone would have to call you the n-word or something that obvious to constitute a solid case of discrimination.

"This all changed in the nineties," he said. "Judges started to realize that no one was going to do things that are overtly and obviously discriminatory. So the burden of proof is predicated on whether or not someone is a member of a protected class, can prove substantial harm by the actions taken against them, and whether they can prove differential treatment based on race, ethnicity, etc." This does not make it easy to prove discrimination, but it gave me a measuring stick to use with my situation.

I decided that I would be willing to sue the school board if they terminated my contract for the reasons that they stated. I knew that I could prove that I had been repeatedly treated in an inherently unfair and inferior manner.

When Peggy told our son Thomas about my decision he said, "This is completely out of character for Dad!"

"I know," she said, "but he needs to stand up for himself. Some of the things that are happening to him don't make any sense. He is getting a lawyer because they got an attorney and did not tell him what the issue was. He honestly doesn't know what this is about."

"Dad never sues anyone!" Tom said. "He plays by a set of rules that nobody plays by anymore!"

"He has finally caught on," she said.

One night as I was praying before going to bed I started to laugh out loud at the irony of my situation. I was about to be kicked to the curb while God was increasing my stature and reputation in the eyes of others. Through my monthly *Thompson Talk Videos* online I found a real bond with students. (These videos were character lessons in which I would relate a story about a famous person, my family growing up, poetry, or literature in order to encourage them to develop good character.) A legendary former superintendent told me that he thought I was the best superintendent in the district since his tenure. This was gratifying but far from vindication.

My laughter led to tears as I thanked God for His blessings. I do not subscribe to the theology that everything happens for a reason or that everything that happens is God's will. I do, however, subscribe to the theology of Romans 8:28, which states, "And we know that God causes all things to work together for good to those who love God, to those who are called according to His purpose" (NAS). I do not believe for one moment that God was jerking the rug out from underneath me to teach me some lesson. I do believe that God uses even the strangest and even most unjust circumstances for my good. I didn't fully understand what I was going through, but I put my absolute trust in Him, knowing that He is good.

Eventually I was placed on administrative leave, and finally the school district and I reached an agreement, but I still felt uneasy. I regretted that I did not move forward with a lawsuit. However, the expense would have been prohibitive, and it might have taken several years to recover lost wages. I applied for a few positions in the state of Wisconsin but did not get any interviews. I was told that part of the cause was that the reasons for my termination were posted on the Internet due to the open records law, which makes any action by a school board a public record. I was constrained by the agreement that I signed from giving my full rebuttal to all of the assertions. If the paper had published my response it would have contained most of the assertions that I would have used in a lawsuit. The publishing of my response defending me from the allegations against me would have helped to answer the questions about why I was being let go. It would have cast some question on whether or not other agendas were being played out. The positive of doing this had to be weighed against the potential consequence. Since I required another job, casting a negative light upon the school board of that district would have only hurt me. There would have been no crowd cheering me for my verbal vindication. Instead, my application for any other job would have found its way into the circular file. The new district would have surmised that, given similar circumstances, I would do the same to them.

After a few months and with the help of a friend who worked for a search firm I was able to interview for a position as an interim superintendent. I was fortunate to be hired, and they accepted my explanation about why I settled with my previous agreement as part of a buyout. I hope that this does not become an impediment going forward.

Though these current circumstances make it seem that I have an uncertain future somewhat impacted by the incident I have recounted in this chapter, nothing could be farther from the truth. I must finish this chapter by saying that throughout my lifetime I have experienced the unmerited favor and grace of God in immeasurable ways. Some of the stories that I have shared in this book are testimonies to His grace. I have seen God open doors for me that were beyond my wildest expectations. I have trusted Him to counteract anything that was meant to harm me and to neutralize any weapons that were formed against me. I have never believed that any human hindrance gets the final say as to the direction and opportunities that lay ahead for me. He gets to say the amen to my life and story. In Jeremiah 29:11 it says, "'For I know the plans I have for you,' declares the LORD, 'plans to prosper you and not to harm you, plans to give you hope and a future'" (NIV). I know that a bright future awaits me and that it is one that I can excitedly wait to enter.

EPILOGUE

WHEN I FIRST started writing my story I thought it would be a labor of love. It became much more than that. Although I was prepared to examine my memories and convey my experiences, I wasn't expecting to relive the emotions that accompanied them. On some of the pages of this book I shed many tears. This surprised me. I really thought I'd dealt with these issues, but I discovered instead that I've repressed many of my feelings and, in truth, I've lived in denial about the impact of race upon my life. I've tried to live above the potentially negative effects of racism, putting things behind me, or so I thought. But unexpected things have opened a torrent of feelings in me during the writing of this book.

Having a bachelor's degree in history, I enjoy reading history books for leisure, and one day as I sat in our high school library waiting to visit a classroom I was reading *Team of Rivals* by Doris Kearns Goodwin. This book highlights the leadership and the character of Abraham Lincoln and tells about the advisors he surrounded himself with during the Civil War. As I began to read the chapter on the fight surrounding the passing of the Thirteenth Amendment to the Constitution, making slavery illegal in the United States, the story drew me in, and tears began to flow from my eyes. It was as if I were a part of the drama of this all-important amendment. I wasn't just reading a piece of history; I was reading a part of the narrative of my ancestors' story. These events have had a direct impact on my own life—past, present, and future.

Through this journey I've learned a very important lesson about walking with God as a Christian: God isn't into denial. He specializes in reality. Even God cannot help you to confront areas in your life that need healing if you choose to live in fantasy or denial. He insists that you look life square in the face. When it gets overwhelming and we cry out to Him for help, He is more than happy to step in and help. I have spent more time in prayer as my repressed feelings have surfaced. I have had to confess some bitterness toward those who have hurt me and accept that I have been placed in many of these situations because He is preparing me for situations that demand a forgiving spirit.

I have a feeling that I will always be in situations where I am one of the few men of my color in leadership. It is a tough and lonely place to be. I just hope that I am someone else's forerunner, blazing a trail for them to follow and opening the door of opportunity for them. Someday some black man will be able to sit in a meeting of educational leaders and not think about being the only one in the room because they won't be the only one, or even one of the few. When that happens we will truly be making progress where race is concerned.

I want to finish this book with a few prescriptions about how to move forward toward racial understanding and healing.

Take the lead

Given my age, I can remember the hesitancy of the evangelical church to become involved in the civil rights movement. Many were concerned about losing their focus on Christ and being drawn into what was called the social gospel, as some mainline churches had. I understand that concern; even today there are churches that speak out about social issues but fail to proclaim the gospel of Jesus Christ. In spite of all of this, however, the true church must speak out against injustice. The church is to be salt and light, but if our only impact is upon those who live in the salt shaker or under the lampshade we have become impotent and irrelevant.

The road to racism is an obstacle course that zigzags between issues of crime, poverty, culture, history, religion, education, and fear. If we're going to continue to make progress as a society we've got to travel this road with honesty, unity, and a spirit of forgiveness. As Christ-followers we must lead the national conversation and set an example of God's love for all people. After all, didn't the Savior come to redeem the human race? Revelation 5:9–10 shows a beautiful picture of our hope: "You are worthy to take the scroll and to open its seals, because you were slain, and with your blood you purchased for God persons from every tribe and language and people and nation. You have made them to be a kingdom and priests to serve our God, and they will reign on the earth" (NAS).

Build relationships

If you really care about improving race relations you must realize that change is born out of relationships. Let me share the story of a long journey toward friendship that happened between a boy from western Pennsylvania and myself.

I was in seventh grade when I first met Billy (not his real name). My teacher came to me and said that Billy was a shy kid who had just moved to Wisconsin and asked if

I could make him feel welcome. Please excuse me if this sounds offensive, but Billy seemed like a hillbilly to me. His thick accent made him hard to understand at first. I agreed to take him under my wing. I thought I was going to do a good deed for a short while and then Billy would become someone else's project. That did not happen.

We became friends and remained friends over the years. We joked about everything, including race and our divergent cultures. When we were about twenty years old Billy paid me what he thought was the highest compliment that he could give me. He said, and I quote, "Milt, you're a good nigger!" I was shocked. It must have been the early 1970s. I wanted to knock him out, but I noticed something. He wasn't using the word with any degree of malice. Given where and how he grew up it was the only way that he knew how to express his feelings.

Of course, I rebuked him and told him not to ever use that word again, and he gave me a sincere, heartfelt apology. I accepted it, and our friendship moved forward. In time I would be his confidant and his pastor and helped him through some hard times. We remained friends for several decades. He changed my life, and I changed his.

I tell this story so that you will understand that if you are easily offended you will never have meaningful relationships with other human beings, whether they are of a different race or not. Real relationships require time, lots of conversations, and understanding.

When I first met one of my college friends it was a culture shock for both of us. He was white and from the small, rural community of Argyle, Wisconsin. I was black and from a much larger Wisconsin city. I actually asked him if they made argyle socks there. He said no. I look back now and think of how stupid that question was, but that's the point! When you first build a friendship with someone from a different racial or ethnic group there are going to be some stupid questions asked and a lot of misinformation. Blacks who live in New York may not know what questions to ask of a white person growing up in Jackson Hole, Wyoming. That's natural and that's fine; stupid questions come with the territory. My friend had stereotypes about me too since he never had a black friend before. He was a great friend. We shared pizza and laundry money together, and I learned a lot from him.

There are differences between today's politically correct world and the environment I experienced growing up in the 1960s, seventies, and eighties. Back then we talked about race. We joked about race. One of my favorite movies is *Blazing Saddles* by Mel Brooks. Its use of racial invectives to drive home the point of the story is done in a way that caused people to laugh their way into awareness. Other films, like *Watermelon Man* and *Black Like Me,* explored the uncomfortable topic of racism using terminology that exposed the prejudice hidden within many human beings.

Contrast this with today's fragile environment where people would rather say nothing than say something unintentionally offensive. That's partly why race relations are moving backward. So here's my advice for people of my own race: Don't take yourself so seriously that you can't entertain questions about the music you listen to or the foods you eat. Don't be offended when people ask questions about the number of black babies that are born out of wedlock or other sensitive issues. Instead try to be understanding and appreciate the courage of those who care enough to risk being called a racist by you. I applaud them. Who knows, it could lead to some pretty good life-long friendships and great conversations.

Dare to forgive

Many of my life experiences have opened my eyes to my need to react differently to potential racism. After experiencing the loss of a job that I believe was the result of discrimination I was very angry at first, knowing I'd been treated differently from whites who had held my position previously. Even though I felt justified in my anger I knew that as a Christian I could not walk in unforgiveness. However, I found that forgiveness is a lot harder than I'd thought, even though I had prayed and made a conscious decision not to hold a grudge.

It wasn't until I attended a state educational conference that reality hit. Several of my former employers walked past me as I was sitting down during a break. They smiled and waved at me, but I did not wave back. I was shocked by their hypocrisy. How could they accuse me of the things that they did and then smile and act as if nothing happened?

Throughout the rest of the conference I avoided them. I did not want to acknowledge them, and they also avoided me. I had that sick feeling you get when you're harboring anger and hurt. I forgot that sometimes forgiveness is not as easy as just snapping your fingers. I have gone to the Lord, and with His help I will truly forgive them. When that happens I will know it because there won't be any shame on my part. The whole ordeal will be just a bad memory and a temporary obstacle in my life.

I share this experience to give an essential piece of advice to blacks who have experienced discrimination. It is imperative that you forgive those who have tried to take your dignity through their action. Jesus demanded that we forgive others if we expect the forgiveness of our heavenly Father. I know firsthand how difficult this can be, but I refuse to allow the cancer of bitterness to possess me. God has a purpose for me that is too valuable to sacrifice for the sake of revenge and hatred. My ancestors suffered through much more than I will ever face. They did it with grace, dignity, and forgiveness. I want to be worthy of being their descendant.

Promote freedom of speech

In today's world of political correctness and safe speech zones the right to have an opinion about many topics is being driven underground, race notwithstanding. But regulating speech doesn't change the heart. The more we restrict free speech, the deeper our thoughts and frustrations are buried. Eventually they explode like a volcano, as we've seen in places like Ferguson, Missouri, even overflowing to a national level.

However, meaningful conversations will never happen if you just talk past people and dig in your heels on issues. Discussions about race are messy because they are charged with emotion, but name-calling and over-the-top rhetoric diminishes credibility and open-mindedness. Sometimes the talk is rocky and leads to temporary misunderstanding, but sometimes it leads people to an epiphany. When a light comes on they begin to see other people through different eyes.

As I explained in Chapter 2, a school board member in Madison, Wisconsin, stated publicly that poverty does not adequately explain the differences in student achievement. He stated that race has to be part of the reason for the differences in student achievement between black and white children. He came to this conclusion by comparing the achievement of black kids who were from middle- and upper-class backgrounds to those of white kids of the same socioeconomic level. I read the comments that accompanied this news story with great interest. I have been arguing this point for the last few years with educators who have abandoned race as a factor and have embraced only discussions on poverty.

While some people called him crazy and questioned his integrity, I wanted to applaud his courage and his honesty. He took a risk by publicly stating this opinion, acknowledging that there are still lingering effects to racism, even when there is no longer any legal discrimination at play. That's what makes this problem much harder to fix.

Become a champion

There are many dedicated parents in the black community who care deeply about their children's education and their future. But for other black children, to make the American dream real they will need champions. For those who are not fortunate enough to have strong family support, the caring adults they find at school or in the community at large can offset this deficit. An example of this is my own wife, who has committed her career to becoming a champion for these children.

When Peggy first arrived as a teacher at Bose Elementary School in Kenosha, Wisconsin, she saw that there were desks placed outside of certain classrooms in the hallway. Whenever a student was disruptive they were put out in the hallway to sit by themselves. She noticed that many of the occupants of these desks were little black boys. Some of these boys were naughty, and though they were hard to teach, few had anyone stepping forward to be their champion. You see, to teach this kind of student takes real commitment. It is easy to succeed with compliant students who come to school from middle- and upper-class homes, ready-made for success. But the prerequisite for success with these students is often for them to know that you care about them and you won't give up on them. They will test you at every turn to see whether you are for real or not. Some teachers do not pass the test.

There are many things that I admire about Peggy, but no reason ranks higher than her commitment to be a champion, especially for African-American males. I think she sees Nate in the faces of many of those young men. Having experience with our own sons, Peggy showed them that she cared and told these boys that she wanted them to succeed just like she wanted her own sons, who are black, to succeed. Her dedication helped build relationships with the parents as well as the students because they knew she understood how they felt. Advocating for them with other teachers, even as they moved along to higher grades, helped them to dream and refuse to settle for low expectations in life. That's what a champion does. I have seen some of these children say hello to my wife while we've been out to eat, hugging her and thanking her for the role that she played in their lives and success. She downplays her role. They do not.

There were other practices at the school that involved giving students lower grades if they did remedial work. Peggy stood against this as blatantly unfair. These students entered school showing lower achievement than their more affluent peers and were given remedial work to help them catch up. Instead of recognizing that all children don't learn at the same pace and encouraging them by grading their efforts commensurate with their new and improving grade levels, the system was reinforcing their academic inferiority and discouraging the effort needed to catch them up. Some thought the solution was to cap the grades that these students could earn when doing remedial work, but this was punishing the victim. These students did not control their circumstances of poverty or their parents' value of education. Why not reward their work at each step and watch them attain grade-level work? The assistant superintendent of instruction at that time agreed with Peggy's proposal, and the practice was not allowed to continue.

Christian businessmen and women can also become champions for children and young adults. The solution to the staggering unemployment rates for African-American males and females does not lie with the government; it lies with individuals. If Christian business leaders would commit to mentoring even just one young man or woman who needs to be championed, it would make a significant difference. It would take patience and the willingness to teach someone both job skills and life skills, but the payoff would be well worth that sacrifice. In this way the church can help change the life of a generation of students who are the downtrodden, some of whom are part of a permanent underclass.

My hope is that followers of Christ will become courageous about tackling racial and ethnic issues. Jesus addresses prejudice through the parable of the good Samaritan. In the biblical story a man is beaten and robbed and left for dead along a road. Various people walk by him, not caring to help him until a stranger, a Samaritan who is considered an ethnic enemy, stops to bandage his wounds and take him away to be cared for. I am not such a victim, but I wonder how many good Samaritans there are who notice those who have been beaten and left for dead by a society that has ceased to pay attention.

Be intentional about integration

It's time for all vestiges of racial separation to cease, especially in the church. The fact that we can refer to white churches and black churches is a shame and, I am sure, displeasing to the Lord Jesus Christ. How this voluntary segregation aligns with Scripture I do not understand. Some say that this is just a matter of cultural preference, that blacks prefer to worship with other blacks and whites with other whites. But if you carry this thinking back in time you would realize that Jews in the early church preferred to worship with Jews and Gentiles with Gentiles, but God had other ideas! The church at Antioch in the Book of Acts was made up of both Jews and Gentiles and serves as an example for the body of Christ and the kingdom of God.

Pastors, have you ever held joint worship services with other churches as a step toward reconciliation? I have seen this happen, and it focuses us on the Lord and His priorities. If your church begins to open up to people of other races and ethnic groups, be aware that people may be overly self-conscious at first. Your overtures at friendliness may be met with a little standoffish response at first, even though your efforts are sincere. But the fruit of such relationships can be extremely rewarding, if not life-changing. I have experienced this firsthand and want to share with you how it changed my life.

When I was a child I attended St. John's Methodist Church in Racine, Wisconsin. It was an all-black congregation on Silver Street in a part of the city that today would be categorized as the ghetto. This was the 1960s, and racial segregation was the norm in the church. But then a mind-blowing change came about.

The Conference of the Methodist Church in Wisconsin determined that radical steps needed to be taken to combat racial segregation within the church. A dialogue regarding a church merge began to take place between the pastor of St. John's, Earnest Lofton, and the young pastor of Bethel Swedish Methodist Church, Don Fadner. They worked through many details and presented a plan to each of the congregations about the merge. The greatest opposition came from the Swedish Methodist Church, but the merge went forward.

Blending the two cultures was very interesting. We had a chancel choir that sang traditional church music and a gospel choir that sang spirituals and traditional black gospel music. The church dinners were fascinating mixtures of ethnic foods. But while this church stood out in its dedication to counter racial segregation by worshiping God together, there were underlying issues. I remember the trouble began when most of us kids became teenagers.

I was made president of the youth group. I wish I could tell you that we sat around and studied the Bible, but instead we would meet and play juvenile games like *kiss, slap, and hug*. Sadly, as friendships developed into dating during the teen years, members of the congregation who were afraid that their children would engage in interracial dating left abruptly.

Nevertheless, news of our unique church spread outside of Racine. Somehow, Martin Luther King Sr. heard about it and said that he wanted to see it for himself. When he visited the church he was impressed with our history-making breakthrough of blacks and whites worshiping together.

This story would be spectacular enough if it ended here, but there is more. A few years later, after Pr. Lofton was kicked upstairs (promoted within the denomination, not to heaven) and Pr. Fadner had moved on, a new pastor arrived. Vincent Sammartino was a Spirit-filled Italian pastor who preached the gospel with a passion. He also had a beautiful, operatic voice. When he sang, the rafters shook.

The Methodist Conference intervened again and determined that another merger was called for. The leaders had their eye on another Methodist church on the other side of town—a congregation that had been birthed in the early 1900s during the time of the Pentecostal Revival. In that day, when some Italian Catholics from nearby Kenosha experienced the baptism of the Holy Spirit, they started a mission church in Racine that eventually became a Methodist church.

The merger plan went ahead, and this time there was no great exodus of members; the Italians in the Racine–Kenosha area understood the sting of discrimination, having experienced it themselves a generation before. For most, worshiping with black brothers and sisters was not a problem.

In time there was a blending of cultures and friendships at a level I had not witnessed in the earlier merge. The black gospel choir started to gain white members, one of whom became special to me in time. It was Mavis Might, who later became my mother-in-law. The chancel choir also became integrated. It wasn't forced or mandated; it was just the natural progression of things for people of God who learned to love one another. The church dinners were spectacular celebrations of Italian and soul food, each partaking of one another's cultural dishes. Folks sat around enjoying coffee and donuts together after service each week. Some of the men would sit and swap stories, and many of them became close friends outside of church. Charles Might, my future father-in-law, and Arzell Thompson, my dad, became lifelong friends during this period of time.

It was in this context that I met my beautiful wife, Peggy. As I write this I am impressed by the love of God shared across racial lines and His providence in bringing me and my wife together. To top off this wonderful story, the church was located on Harmony Drive.

This slice of history illustrates what is still possible today. The talk of cultural barriers and other boundaries is an unacceptable impediment if we are to truly live out what the Bible teaches and set an example for our weary world. To me, they are the excuses that are imposed when God calls us to do something that makes our human nature uncomfortable. As a Christian I am not aware that making my human nature comfortable is of primary concern.

We live in a world that appears to be getting darker. The ability to make and keep relationships across human divisions seems to be getting harder and harder. The church is getting lighter and lighter, however. I know that if the Holy Spirit is allowed to change us, changing our perspective from the view of earthly citizenship to that of being heavenly citizens who demonstrate how people relate to one another in heaven, we will bring about tremendous change. We will be living out the covenant relationship of the kingdom of God and healing divisions of every kind. This is not just my dream. It is my mission.

NOTES

CHAPTER 2:
THE SUPERFICIAL WOUND

1. "Percentage of population in the United States in 2014 and 2060, by race and Hispanic origin," *Statista, The Statistics Portal.* Accessed April 13, 2016, at http://www.statista.com/statistics /270272/percentage-of-us-population-by-ethnicities/.

2. Wisconsin Association of School District Administrators Conference (Madison, WI: September 25, 2014).

CHAPTER 12:
IRISH FOR GOOD MEASURE

1. "CNN Pilot Demonstration 4-28-10," *CNN*, April 28, 2010. Accessed April 13, 2016, at http://i2.cdn.turner.com/cnn/2010 /images/05/13/expanded_results_methods_cnn.pdf.

2. "Semester Enrollments by Diversity," *Office of the Registrar, University of Wisconsin–Madison.* Accessed April 14, 2016, at https://registrar.wisc.edu/semester_enrollments_by_diversity.htm.

3. "University of Wisconsin–Madison College Portrait," *College Portrait.* Accessed April 13, 2016, at http://www.collegeportraits .org/WI/UW-Madison.

4. "Population of Wisconsin: Census 2010 and 2000 Interactive Map, Demographics, Statistics, Quick Facts," *CensusViewer.* Accessed April 13, 2016, at http://censusviewer.com/state/WI.

5. UW–Milwaukee data available at "University of Wisconsin–Madison College Portrait," *College Portrait.* Data about the city of Milwaukee available at "Milwaukee, Wisconsin Population: Census 2010 and 2000 Interactive Map, Demographics, Statistics, Quick Facts," *CensusViewer.* Accessed April 13, 2016, at http:// censusviewer.com/city/WI/Milwaukee.

CHAPTER 13:
MY BROTHERS AND THE SUCCESS OF MY FAMILY

1. Walter E. Williams, "The True Black Tragedy: Illegitimacy Rate of Nearly 75%," *CNS News*, May 19, 2015. Accessed April 14, 2016, at http://www.cnsnews.com/commentary/walter-e-williams /true-black-tragedy-illegitimacy-rate-nearly-75.

2. Ibid. See also Center for Disease Control, "Births: Final Data for 2014," *National Vital Statistics Reports* 64, no. 12 (2015): 4. Accessed April 13, 2016, at http://www.cdc.gov/nchs/data/nvsr/nvsr64/nvsr64_12.pdf.

3. For more information visit Jaime Diaz, *The New York Times*, September 11, 1990. Accessed April 13, 2016, at http://www.nytimes.com/1990/09/11/sports/augusta-national-admits-first-black-member.html.

Chapter 14:
Justice and the Lens of Race

1. Eric Malnic, "The Simpson Verdicts: Shapiro Trades Criticism with Cochran and Bailey," *Los Angeles Times*, October 4, 1995, available at https://owl.english.purdue.edu/owl/resource/717/04/.

Chapter 15:
Progress and the Unfinished Work

1. The transcript of this seminal speech is available at Martin Luther King Jr., "I Have a Dream" (Washington, DC, August 28, 1963). Accessed April 12, 2016, at https://www.archives.gov/press/exhibits/dream-speech.pdf.

2. *Race: The Power of an Illusion*, produced by Larry Adelman (2003; San Francisco: California Newsreel). Information on this segment is available at "Go Deeper: Where Race Lives," *PBS.org*, 2003, http://www.pbs.org/race/000_About/002_06_b-godeeper.htm.

3. Dan Harris and Gitika Ahuja, "Race for a Cab: When Hailing a Ride Isn't So Black and White," *ABC News*, April 1, 2009. Accessed April 14, 2016, at http://abcnews.go.com/GMA/race-cab-hailing-ride-black-white/story?id=7223511.

4. Ibid.

5. Bernie Augustine, "Mavericks owner Mark Cuban offers apology to Trayvon Martin's family after making 'black kid in a hoodie' remark," *New York Daily News*, May 23, 2014. Accessed April 11, 2016, at http://www.nydailynews.com/sports/basketball/cuban-prejudice-article-1.1801985.

6. Ibid.

ABOUT THE AUTHOR

Milt Thompson is an educator and a pastor. He has had a great educational career as a teacher, principal, and superintendent of schools. He formerly pastored Omega Christian Fellowship from 1983 to 2002. He is currently pastor of Living Stones Charismatic Fellowship in Racine, Wisconsin. It is a church that focuses on teaching the Word in an understandable manner, moving in gifts of the Holy Spirit, and simple praise.

Milt has been married to Margaret (Peggy) Thompson for forty years. They have four sons, Nathanael, Matthew, Thomas, and Daniel.

Milt has been a keynote speaker at national and state conferences. He is available as a speaker and presenter at conferences and as a guest speaker for church services.

CONTACT THE AUTHOR

Milt Thompson can be contacted at
miltministries@gmail.com.
His website is livingstonescharismatic.com,
on which he posts a blog and teachings.